Making Money Work

Careers & the New Economy

Gen Z Guide to Financial Intelligence

James Minter

Part of the

Eyes-Wide-Open Book Series

www.jamesminter.com

MINTER PUBLISHING LIMITED

Minter Publishing Limited (MPL)
3 Coach House Mews
Cheltenham, GL50 2AU

Copyright © James Minter 2025

James Minter has asserted his rights under the
Copyright, Design, and Patents Act, 1988
to be the author of this work

eBook ISBN: 978-1-910727-65-2
Paperback ISBN: 978-1-910727-64-5

Printed and bound in Great Britain by Ingram Spark,
Milton Keynes.

This book is sold subject to the condition that it shall not, by way of trade or otherwise, be lent, resold, hired out, or otherwise circulated in any form of binding or cover other than that in which it is published and without a similar condition, including this condition, being imposed on the subsequent purchaser.

CONTENTS

PREFACE I
INTRODUCTION: YOUR FINANCIAL FREEDOM 1
THE MONEY MINDSET 5
FINANCIAL LITERACY 101 19
YOUR UK BANK ACCOUNT 31
CREDIT SCORES AND CREDIT CARDS EXPLAINED 43
MONEY-SAVING STRATEGIES 55
BUILDING YOUR FINANCIAL FUTURE 67
FROM COLLEGE TO APPRENTICESHIPS TO SELF-TAUGHT 81
EARNING IN THE AGE OF AI: JOBS, GIGS, & SIDE HUSTLES 89
PROTECTING YOUR WEALTH 107
THE UK TAX SYSTEM BASICS 113
NEGOTIATION & VALUE-BASED THINKING 123
THRIVING IN UNCERTAIN TIMES 131
MONEY, ETHICS, & SOCIAL GOOD 139
THE FUTURE - RETIREMENT & LEGACY 147
CONCLUSION 152
FURTHER READING BY TOPIC 156
BOOK REVIEW REQUEST 159
TITLES IN THE 'EYES-WIDE-OPEN' SERIES 160
ABOUT THE AUTHOR 164
SOCIAL MEDIA 165
ACKNOWLEDGEMENTS 166

The information contained in this book is for educational purposes only and shouldn't be regarded as financial advice.

Of Money - by Barnabe Googe

Money, thou bane of bliss, and source of woe,
Thou cause of all our quarrel, and distress,
Money, thou root of hate, and endless strife,
Yet, must we love thee, though thou spoil our life.

This poem, dating back to the 16th century, succinctly captures the paradox of money: it's both coveted and a cause of turmoil, compelling affection even as it brings trouble.

> *Remember: "Spending is easy, earning is hard; don't forget which one builds your future."*

PREFACE

Gen Z refers to people born between 1997 and 2012, which means the age range of this group is 13 to 28 at the time of writing. If you're a young teenager (13–17), this book opens a window into your financial and working future. It helps you see how money, careers, and opportunities may shape your life as you grow older. Inside, you'll discover real-life stories, practical insights, and honest reflections on the choices you'll face, from earning your first pay to building long-term financial independence. Think of it as your personal roadmap to navigating money, work, and the future that lies ahead.

For those of you aged 18 to 24 who are entering adulthood, starting careers, and making life-shaping decisions, this book is designed with your financial and professional future in mind. Inside, you'll find practical strategies, fresh ideas, and tools to help you take control of your money, navigate the world of work, and prepare for what's ahead. Whether it's setting financial goals, building resilience in uncertain job markets, or creating a career with purpose, this guide is your companion for taking the next confident step forward.

And if you're at the upper end of the Gen Z age range (25–28), already gaining work and financial experience, this book offers an opportunity to pause and reflect on how you're doing and your future direction. These chapters will help you reassess your financial habits, refine your career skills, and strengthen your independence. From tackling new financial challenges to exploring strategies for long-term stability and growth, there is always more to learn and adopt as you continue to build a prosperous future.

In an era marked by rapid technological change and an abundance of information, thoughtful curation is essential for genuine understanding. Each book in this series has been developed through dedicated literature research, leveraging advanced tools such as Perplexity to ensure that every topic is presented with clarity, accuracy, and relevance.

The materials in this book are carefully organised to create a thorough learning journey. Throughout each chapter, you will find not only insightful content but also practical exercises designed to strengthen your understanding. This hands-on approach is especially tailored for Gen Z readers, enabling you to engage with concepts and apply them in real-world situations in a meaningful way.

Our goal is to inspire curiosity, foster critical thinking, and equip you with skills that matter now and in the future. By combining the best research with interactive learning, the Eyes-Wide-Open book series is designed to empower individuals to acquire knowledge and equip themselves with the tools necessary to make informed decisions about their future. We invite you to explore, question, and grow, keeping your eyes wide open to the possibilities ahead.

INTRODUCTION: YOUR FINANCIAL FREEDOM

Whether you're just starting out or aiming to improve your money management skills, this book will equip you with the knowledge, tools, and strategies to take control of your finances, build lasting wealth, and work confidently towards financial freedom.

Inside, you'll learn how to:

- Understand the psychology of money and rewrite limiting beliefs
- Budget with purpose and align spending with your values
- Save strategically and protect your financial future
- Invest wisely and harness the power of compounding
- Create passive income streams and diversify your earnings
- Utilise financial tools to optimise your potential and remain motivated

But more than just practical advice, this book encourages a mindset change. It inspires you to see money not as a source of stress or confusion, but as a tool for freedom, impact, and self-expression. It's about building a life where your finances support your dreams, rather than limit them.

Whether your aim is to travel the world, support your family, start a business, or simply enjoy a better night's sleep knowing you're financially secure, this book is here to help you achieve it.

Why Money Matters, But Doesn't Define You

In modern economies, money greatly influences almost every part of daily life. It decides where you live, what you eat, the experiences you seek, and even the freedom to refuse something that doesn't benefit you. Understanding money, how to earn, save, invest, and protect it isn't about greed. It's about agency. It's about recognising that you're not at the mercy of a broken system or random chance. It's about reclaiming time, freedom, and peace of mind.

But here's the truth: you only get one life. No amount of money can buy back wasted time, repair neglected health, or replace meaningful moments missed chasing someone else's definition of success. Financial intelligence matters, but it should fuel your life, not consume it.

Right now, you might just want to explore, gain independence, and have fun, and you absolutely should. Your current age is for discovering who you are and what lights you up. But here's the imperative: at some stage, sooner than you think, you'll need to put food on your table, keep a roof over your head, and wear clothes that make you feel like yourself. The choices you make about money today will shape your options tomorrow. Money isn't everything, but it's the foundation that supports your freedom, your adventures, and your future security.

The goal isn't to obsessively hoard money or flaunt wealth on social media. It's to use money as a tool, not a measure of your worth. Learn the system, play it smart, and then get back to living. Travel. Laugh. Build. Connect. Be present.

Your value goes way beyond your bank balance. But understanding money now means you'll have the power to write your own story, on your terms.

The foundations of a successful financial journey are awareness, developing thoughtful habits, and shifting mindset. The first chapter explores the myths and realities of wealth, happiness, and status. Turn the page to begin one of the most important journeys you'll ever make.

MASTER YOUR MONEY MINDSET

The Money Mindset

1

THE MONEY MINDSET

Myths and Realities About Wealth, Happiness, and Status

In the UK, as in many other societies, there is a longstanding belief that owning property and earning a high salary are clear signs of success. However, real financial well-being extends far beyond a payslip or postcode. Despite what advertising and even government policy might imply, research increasingly shows that once our basic needs for food, housing, health, and security are met, the link between money and happiness quickly diminishes. The idea that 'money buys happiness' is more myth than fact; happiness tends to level off once incomes cover essential living costs and allow for modest comforts. Focusing solely on prestige or accumulation often leads to "hedonic adaptation", where an increase in income brings progressively less satisfaction over time.

Furthermore, visible wealth and status can conceal deeper realities. Many individuals with flashy lifestyles or designer goods are burdened with significant debts or financial worries. Particularly in cities such as London, Birmingham, and Manchester, the desire to keep up with peers or the 'Instagram elite' can lead to financial choices that undermine long-term stability. For Gen Z, who grapple with high rent, student loans, and uncertain job markets, it's essential to challenge oversimplified narratives: security isn't something you can purchase but an outcome of good habits, healthy mindsets, and realistic expectations.

How Upbringing, Culture, and Social Media Shape Money Beliefs

For most of us, our first lessons about money usually come from our parental home; sometimes through direct conversations, but more often from what's left unsaid. In many UK households, discussing finances openly is still considered impolite or uncomfortable, creating gaps in understanding that persist into adulthood. Family background can greatly influence attitudes towards spending, saving, and risk-taking. For example, children from families facing financial difficulties may develop anxiety about money or adopt a 'save at all costs' outlook, while others might imitate their parents' spendthrift habits.

Modern culture, particularly social media, greatly amplifies these influential forces. Algorithms deliver a constant stream of influencers showcasing luxury holidays, designer fashion, or entrepreneurial 'hustles.' UK-based creators might highlight city living or travel, reinforcing the idea that success is both visible and consumable. Trends such as the FIRE (Financial Independence, Retire Early) movement and 'manifesting money' have gained particular traction among Gen Zers. While these can promote positive habits, they can also create comparison traps. Seeing others' apparent success can cause anxiety, lead us to undervalue our own achievements, or prompt reckless efforts to imitate lifestyles far beyond our means

Rise of Side Hustles & Redefining 'Making It'

The traditional nine-to-five career route, with its promise of steady advancement, is rapidly being replaced or at least supplemented by gig and freelance work among young people. Confronted with stagnant wages and high living expenses, many Gen Z individuals are taking on side jobs for both income and personal fulfilment. These include running Etsy shops, tutoring online, delivering food with services like Deliveroo, or reselling limited-edition trainers. The growth of the gig economy isn't just about making ends meet; for many, it represents a form of empowerment, offering greater flexibility and the opportunity to define success on their own terms.

Instead of chasing promotions or traditional milestones, many young people now prioritise autonomy, meaningful work, and mental well-being. Success might mean having time for passion projects, travelling, or simply maintaining a healthy work-life balance. There is also a new realism: higher education no longer guarantees well-paid jobs, and the UK housing market creates barriers to homeownership for most under-30s. As a result, 'making it' has taken on a much more personal and diverse significance, liberated from one-dimensional measures and centred on living according to one's values and circumstances.

Mindset: Foundation of Your Financial Journey

Your financial journey doesn't start with a paycheque; it begins in your head. Your mindset is the engine behind every financial decision, from how you spend your first £10 to how you invest your first £10,000. A growth-oriented mindset helps you rise above setbacks, break free from destructive habits, and stay focused on achieving long-term financial freedom. But without this internal foundation, even the most detailed budget will crumble under pressure. Shifting how you *think* about money transforms how you *behave* with money.

Habits That Hold You Back

1. Blaming Others or Making Excuses

It's tempting to point fingers when things go wrong financially. You might blame your background, the cost-of-living crisis, or even bad luck. While these factors *do* influence your situation, they don't control your future.

2. Avoiding Financial Literacy

Some people find money tedious or too complex to understand, so they tend to zone out whenever it comes up. But opting out of financial literacy is like stepping into a maze blindfolded; it makes every financial decision riskier.

3. Chasing Approval Over Progress

In today's social media world, image often takes precedence over intention. You might feel pressured to wear designer trainers, upgrade to the latest tech, or dine out often, all just to keep up. However, pursuing validation through spending undermines long-term well-being.

4. Ignoring Personal Growth

Many avoid financial growth because it feels intimidating or irrelevant. But ignoring financial education is like refusing to update your apps: you'll run slower while others progress.

Mindsets That Propel You Forward

1. 'Money Equals Options' - Own It Early

Money is more than just notes and figures; it's an opportunity. It enables you to choose where you live, how you spend your time, and what experiences you pursue. The sooner you recognise this, the more your future will flourish.

2. Set Short-Term Wins & Long-Term Goals

Goals serve as your financial GPS. Without them, you'll drift from payday to payday with no real progress. Short-term wins, like saving £50 a week, build momentum and confidence. Long-term goals, such as saving for a house deposit or a holiday fund, give you purpose.

3. Self-Educate Like a Millionaire

Financial education isn't handed out; you have to claim it. However, you don't need a course or a mentor to get started. Most millionaires learned by reading, watching, listening, and trying. The internet is full of excellent resources, many of which are free.

4. Delayed Gratification: a Gen Z 'Superpower' and How to Build It

Delayed gratification is the ability to resist an immediate reward in favour of a bigger or more meaningful reward in the future. In a fast-paced, instant-everything world, the ability to wait, plan, and work toward longer-term goals truly acts like a 'superpower' for Gen Zers and anyone seeking to achieve financial or personal success.

Common Limiting Beliefs

1. 'Money is Evil'

Many people, especially younger generations, internalise messages like 'money corrupts' or 'rich equals greedy.' These beliefs are often cultural or passed down through generations. But they block progress.

2. 'YOLO Spending'

True, **you only live once,** and living in the moment can feel freeing, but financially, it can leave you trapped. Short-term spending splurges (that £100 night out or £4 daily coffees) feel harmless individually, but compound over time.

3. 'Setbacks Equal Failure'

Financial setbacks hurt. Unexpected bills, job loss, and investment losses can be particularly painful. But failing *once* doesn't mean you've failed *forever*.

Habits That Drive Results

1. Set Achievable Goals

Massive goals without structure can feel overwhelming. Breaking them down makes them doable. Want to save £10K? £200/month for 50 months makes it manageable. Want to pay off debt? Track it weekly and celebrate small wins. Clarity breeds progress, and progress builds belief.

2. Build Micro-Habits

Small habits often outperform drastic changes. Saving £50 a week may seem trivial, but that totals £2,600 in a year. Regularly reviewing your spending, say every Sunday for just 10 minutes, helps build awareness. Recently, I saw two Gen Zers who had diligently saved all their loose change for over three years before taking it to the bank for sorting and counting. The total came to over £5,000. Their Maldives holiday is now a reality.

3. Surround Yourself with Financial Positivity

Your circle shapes your mindset. If your crews always broke by the 15th or dodging debt collectors, it's time to shift. Follow money mentors on TikTok, find financial communities on Instagram, and join budgeting groups on Reddit. Surround yourself with people who ask, "How can I grow?" instead of "How can I spend?"

4. Celebrate Mini Wins

Progress deserves recognition. If you save £1,000, don't wait for £10K to feel proud. Celebrate with a treat, such as dinner, a book, or a movie. It reinforces motivation and reminds you that consistency matters. Wins, no matter how small, deserve joy.

Final Takeaway

Your mindset is the real minimum viable product (MVP) of your money story. The concept of an MVP encourages learning and building with scalability in mind. With an MVP, you're building the first small step at a low risk to your wallet, allowing you to test, refine, and grow step-by-step. You'll start with small steps. This will help you to identify areas where you need to make improvements, scale back, or even add extra actions to increase your success. MVP shapes your habits, decisions, and direction. By owning your attitude toward money, embracing learning, growth, and discipline, you unlock true freedom.

> ### Exercises
>
> The basis for a successful financial journey is awareness, developing mindful habits, and making mindset changes. Use the lined paper at the end of this chapter to write down your answers:
>
> 1. **Recognise Limiting Beliefs**
>
>   Do you have any thoughts that convince you money is scarce, unattainable, or that you don't deserve financial success?
>
>   Choose one limiting belief you've identified in yourself and write a positive, empowering alternative. For example, replace "I will never be good at managing money" with "I am ready to learn and improve my money skills starting today."
>
> 2. **Identify Your Money Habits**
>
>   Take a moment to reflect on your current daily habits related to money. Are you tracking spending and saving, even small amounts?
>
>   Write down two habits you currently practice that help your financial well-being and one habit you feel you need to change.

> **3. Set a Small Intention**
> Based on this reflection, set one small, specific financial habit to practice this week. It might be as simple as reading a short article about money each day.

In the next chapter, you will learn why budgeting and saving are vital for financial stability. Without a plan for your finances, it's easy to lose track of where your money is going and harder to achieve your goals. The next chapter will help you understand the importance of budgeting, recognise common pitfalls, and develop habits that secure your financial future.

Financial Literacy 101

2

FINANCIAL LITERACY 101

Please note that these topics are covered in more detail throughout the book.

What Drains You

1. Not Saving or Budgeting at All

Financial independence starts with understanding how money flows in and out of your life. Budgeting, often seen as boring, is actually empowering. It's about knowing what you have, what you need, and what you want. In the UK, a common rule is the 50/30/20 method: dividing 50% of income to needs (rent, living expenses, utilities), 30% to wants (eating out, streaming, designer clothes), and 20% to savings or debt repayment.

2. Letting Spending Spiral Out of Control

Disorganised spending results in wasted money and missed opportunities to save. You should take steps to control your spending by writing down your monthly income and fixed expenses (such as rent, utility bills, etc.). Then subtract fixed expenses from your income to determine your 'disposable income.' Decide how much of that you will spend, save, and invest, and stick to your plan. Remember, you choose your spending habits, but be mindful of unhealthy ones like smoking, gambling, excessive drinking, and recreational drugs.

What Empowers You

1. Save Before You Spend

The key to building wealth is prioritising saving. Instead of spending first and saving whatever's left, flip the script: save first, then spend the rest guilt-free.

2. Live Under Your Means

Living below your means doesn't mean depriving yourself; instead, it means spending less than you earn, allowing you to save and invest for the future. It's about making intentional choices.

3. Budgeting Isn't Boring - Being Broke Is

Budgeting gives you control over your money. It's not about restricting yourself; it's about making sure your money works for you. Think of it as a roadmap to your goals.

4. Avoid Lifestyle Creep

Lifestyle creep occurs when your spending increases as your income rises, which can also hinder your financial progress. While it's fine to enjoy your success, upgrading too rapidly can keep you in the same financial situation despite earning more.

For example, if you receive a £500 rise and immediately upgrade your car or wardrobe, it might feel good temporarily, but it ultimately results in no extra savings. Instead of upgrading to a luxury car immediately, consider sticking with your current vehicle and using the additional income to invest or save for a larger goal.

5. Understanding Credit, Debt, & Avoiding Traps

Credit is a double-edged sword: used wisely, it helps build your credit score and opens up options for renting flats or securing loans; if unmanaged, it can lead to serious financial problems. In the UK, your credit rating follows you; missed payments and negative marks can affect your financial prospects for years to come.

Understanding student loans in the UK is also crucial. Unlike typical debts, UK student loans are repaid through the tax system and are written off after a specified number of years. This means the psychological impact can be greater than the actual financial risk for many people. Knowing basics like paying your credit card in full each month and avoiding payday lenders can prevent significant stress later.

6. Assets and liabilities

Assets and liabilities are two key concepts in personal finance, and understanding the difference can help you make better financial decisions.

Assets are tangible or intangible things that have value. They can help you generate income or improve your financial position in the future. Common examples:

- Savings in your bank account.
- Investments (stocks, bonds, crypto).
- Valuable possessions (like a laptop, phone, or even collectables).
- Money others owe you.

Liabilities are amounts you owe, representing debts or obligations that need to be repaid. These reduce your overall wealth. Common examples:

- Student loans.
- Credit card balances.
- Car loans.
- Overdrafts or money you owe to friends /family.

Liabilities tend to cost you money over time, primarily if they accrue interest (such as credit cards or loans).

Having more assets than liabilities means you're building wealth; if your liabilities are larger, you may struggle to get ahead financially.

7. Compound Interest

Compound interest is interest that you earn not just on your initial amount of money (the 'principal'), but also on the interest that accumulates over time. This means your savings grow faster compared to simple interest, where you only earn interest on your original principal.

With compound interest, each year's interest is calculated on a larger amount, which includes your initial money plus any interest already earned. Over time, this snowball effect makes a substantial difference, especially as the longer you leave your money, the more it grows!

8. Learning to Read Financial Statements

Learning to read financial statements involves understanding how to interpret and analyse official documents that show how a person, business, or organisation manages its money. Financial statements are structured records that summarise financial activity and financial health. The main types are:

- Income Statement (Profit & Loss): Shows revenue, expenses, and whether there's a profit or loss over a specific period.

- Balance Sheet: Lists what's owned (assets) and what's owed (liabilities) at a point in time, plus net worth (equity).

- Cash Flow Statement: Tracks cash entering and leaving, helping you see how money is actually moving, not just promised or owed.

Learning to read these means more than spotting numbers. It's about:

- Understanding the relationship between income, spending, assets, and debts.

- Spotting trends, problems, or opportunities, such as overspending, increasing debt, or positive growth.

- Using this skill for personal finances, investing, running a side business, or simply being a more informed consumer.

It's essential to Gen Zers, as they face a rapidly changing world; think side hustles, digital banking, student loans, cryptocurrency, and an uncertain job market. Being able to read financial statements is vital because:

- Personal control helps you manage your own money, including budgeting, identifying bad financial habits, and setting smart goals.

- Business sense: With side hustles and freelance work popular among Gen Z, understanding how to read your own (or someone else's) financials is essential for determining if a business idea is profitable or sustainable.

- Smarter investing: If you want to invest in shares or startups, you need to understand their financial health. This helps you avoid scams or bad investments.

- Better life decisions: Understanding financial statements helps you make choices about jobs, loans, or purchases by seeing the real numbers behind offers or contracts.

- Financial literacy: Employers increasingly look for financially literate young people. These skills set you apart in job interviews or entrepreneurial ventures.

In short, learning to read financial statements empowers Gen Zers to make more informed decisions, avoid debt traps, identify economic opportunities, and take control of their financial future.

Real Life Examples

Example 1: From Overdraft Pitfalls to Saving Smart

Jess, a university student in Leeds, often used her overdraft without recognising the long-term impact. When she added up her fees and interest, she was surprised: £3 a week quickly accumulated to £150 a year. After switching to a digital bank, she set up 'pots' for rent, groceries, and saving for a festival. Automated transfers, clear notifications, and spending limits helped her stay in control and avoid old mistakes.

Example 2: Micro-Saving and 'Rounding Up'

Kiran, a 21-year-old apprentice in London, initially struggled to save any money. Then he activated a 'round-up' feature in his banking app: each time he made a purchase for £2.70, for example, a round-up of 30p was transferred to his savings pot. Over six months, he saved £120, enough for a short holiday with friends, demonstrating that small amounts saved steadily accumulate faster than expected.

Exercises

1. Budget Building Worksheet: Use a spreadsheet, such as Microsoft Excel or Google Sheets, or the lined page at the end of this chapter, and start with your most recent payslip, loan, or allowance.

- List your monthly take-home income (after tax).
- Write out all monthly expenses: rent, utilities, phone, groceries, streaming, etc.
- Determine a realistic savings goal.
- Try the 50/30/20 split: how does it compare to your current spending?

2. Savings Challenge: Set a one-month savings goal. Even if it's just £1 per day, commit to putting it aside in a separate account or 'pot.'

3. Digital Detox Exercise: If you're using a digital payment system, review your past month of digital & contactless payments. Are there purchases you barely remember? What patterns can you spot? Pick one category (e.g., takeaway coffee) and challenge yourself to halve your spending on this item next month.

In the next chapter, you will understand why a bank account is vital to your financial future and the importance of selecting the right one for your needs. The integration of technologies such as contactless payments, smartphone apps, and digital wallets is making life easier and transactions more seamless, but the responsibility to manage your spending still rests with you.

Your UK Bank Account

3

YOUR UK BANK ACCOUNT

Gen Z is transforming the financial sector. They are distinct from other generations because their behaviours and thought patterns have been shaped by growing up in an era of digitalisation and economic volatility. As a digitally native generation, they now constitute the largest age group worldwide, making up nearly 32 per cent of the global population. In the UK alone, over 13 million Gen Z individuals reside in this country, becoming an increasingly influential part of the economy and a vital audience for the financial sector.

Gen Zers have a strong desire for immediacy and are accustomed to being able to do everything on their phones and having information available instantly. This poses a challenge for some legacy banks, where their international payment processes can take up to four working days. Long wait times for bank accounts, loans, and mortgage approvals, as well as ineffective processes, cause frustration. The good news is, UK banks are paying attention, with almost two-thirds viewing Gen Z as crucial to securing their future.

Opening a bank account might sound like just another boring box to tick on the road to adulthood, but in reality, it's one of the smartest moves you can make for your personal independence, no matter if you're 13 or 23. Having your own bank account isn't just about storing money. It's about gaining control of your finances and setting yourself up for the future.

With your bank account, you unlock various ways to spend money smartly. You can shop online or in-store and tap away using **Apple Pay** or **Google Pay**. No more worrying about carrying cash or losing out on the best deals just because you can't pay digitally; it's all handled from your phone or debit card.

One of the most rewarding aspects of having your own current account is building your wealth. Depending on the account, you can earn interest, which means your savings grow over time without any effort. Modern banking apps also enable you to monitor your spending and set savings targets, helping you develop strong money habits from the beginning. These features make budgeting less daunting and more practical.

Another important advantage is that opening a bank account helps you build a financial history. Every financial action, from paying bills on time to saving regularly, adds to your credit record. In the future, this can be very useful when you want to rent a property or even buy something larger, such as a car or a house. Lenders prefer to see that you have managed your money responsibly.

And if you're concerned about safety, UK banks provide reassurance. Through the Financial Services Compensation Scheme (FSCS), your money is protected up to £85,000. So, if anything happens to your bank, your funds will remain secure.

Online Bank Accounts

Online banks mainly operate digitally, usually via smartphone apps. Examples include banks such as **Monzo** and **Starling Bank**. These banks lack physical branches like traditional ones, but you can still access customer support and advice through the app. Additionally, you will receive a sort code and account number along with a physical debit card by post.

Through digital banking, you can set up Standing Orders, Direct Debits, transfer money, and pay bills in the same way that you would with a traditional bank account. The best online banks are free to join, although there are costs for premium products.

Popular Online Bank Accounts

The rise of app-only banking is due to the UK government implementing 'open banking', which requires banks to allow customers to share financial data (such as spending habits, regular payments, bank statements, etc.) with budgeting apps or other banks.

- **Revolut:** Revolut's success with Gen Z comes from addressing real pain points (e.g., high fees, clunky interfaces) while communicating in their language, being digitally, socially, and ethically aware. However, issues like fraud risks and regulatory challenges could threaten its longevity. For Gen Z, Revolut isn't just a bank; it's a lifestyle tool that combines finance with seamless, values-driven experiences they seek.

- **Monzo:** Is a digital-only bank founded in 2015. It focuses on enhancing its technology. Customers can open an account within minutes, receive instant payment notifications, automatically save into 'savings pots', and easily split bills with friends. Monzo is one of the top-rated banks in the UK with over nine million customers. Its key selling points are convenience, simplicity, and collaborating with its community to improve and develop new products.

- **Kroo:** Another fully licensed digital bank with FSCS protection. One thing that sets this bank apart is its sustainable approach to banking, along with the interest paid on your current and savings accounts.

- **Starling:** For a well-rounded current account that uses digital banking, Starling Bank is a great option. Its accounts offer a wide range of features, including overdrafts, savings goals and fee-free spending abroad.

Payments

Dominance of Digital and Contactless Payments

Gen Z's payment habits are defined by digital fluency, debt aversion, and demand for seamless experiences. Businesses must prioritise mobile optimisation, flexible payment options, and ethical alignment to capture this influential demographic.

Gen Z, as digital natives, overwhelmingly prefer digital wallets such as **Apple Pay** and **Google Pay**, as well as contactless cards. With 51% using mobile wallets regularly and 80% favouring tap-to-pay over traditional card swipes, their preference is clear. This aligns with their demand for speed and convenience.

Buy Now, Pay Later (BNPL) Adoption

BNPL services (e.g., **Klarna, Clearpay/Afterpay**) are popular, with 46% of Gen Z using them for budget flexibility. Unlike credit cards, BNPL offers interest-free instalment plans, appealing to their debt-averse mindset.

Cash and Credit Cards

Only 10% of Gen Z rely on cash regularly, while 69% use debit cards to avoid credit card debt. Credit card usage remains at 39%, partly due to mistrust of debt and complex terms. As noted above, cash isn't used often, but there is a sense of control when used, as it provides an immediate indication of what you're spending—you can only spend what's in your pocket.

Cryptocurrency and Emerging Trends

23% of Gen Z own cryptocurrency, reflecting their openness to decentralised finance. Real-time payments and blockchain-based solutions are also gaining traction as Gen Z seeks faster, transparent transactions.

The UK is currently still in the design and consultation phase for a central bank digital currency (CBDC), often referred to as the 'digital pound.' It's not anticipated that it will be released before 2027

Security & Environmental, Social & Governance (ESG) Considerations

While Gen Z prioritises transaction speed, they also value security (**e.g., tokenisation**) and **ESG alignment**; 51% choose providers based on their environmental/social impact

Real Life Example

Olivier just turned 17 and landed her first part-time job at the local café down the street. On her first shift, her manager says, "We'll need your bank details so we can pay you."

That evening, she sat down with her laptop, went to her bank's website, and opened a youth current account in her name. No need to drag her parents along – the process is quick, and within days, she received her own debit card. It works contactlessly, so she can tap to pay for a coffee or lunch, and the mobile banking app shows every transaction in real time.

Exercise: Bank Account Challenge

1. **If you don't yet have one, open an online bank account:**
   - Compare two digital banks (e.g., Monzo vs. Starling). What are their benefits, and what are their most valuable features? Which fits your goals best, and why? Look for: no

monthly fees, mobile banking app, savings tools, overseas spending.

- Get familiar with the interface and locate key sections such as Account Overview, Transaction History, where the Cards and Payments are, etc.

2. **Debit Card and Digital Wallets**

- Add your debit card to use on your phone for Apple Pay or Google Wallet.

- Find out how to activate the card and add it to your preferred payment app.

- List two scenarios where contactless or digital payments could make your life easier.

3. **Smart Spending and Saving**

- Use your mobile banking app to track spending after a week. Categorise your purchases (e.g., food, entertainment, travel).

- Set a savings goal (e.g., £200 for a summer trip) using the app's goal or round-up features.

The next chapter provides insights into what credit scores are, how they are calculated, the impact of your choices, and how to use credit cards wisely, illustrated with practical examples and exercises to facilitate active learning.

Credit Scores and Credit Cards Explained

4

CREDIT SCORES AND CREDIT CARDS EXPLAINED

Among the key financial tools are your credit score and your experience with credit cards. Both are crucial for unlocking life's opportunities: from renting your ideal home to securing the best rates on loans, being approved for a mortgage, or even obtaining certain jobs.

What Exactly is a Credit Score?

When you make purchases that you can't pay for in full immediately, instead, using an overdraft, credit card, or loan to cover the costs, you're actually borrowing money. Before anyone lends you money, they assess your trustworthiness; this is where your credit score comes in.

A credit score is a summary of your borrowing and repayment behaviour, expressed as a three-digit number. It gives potential lenders a quick snapshot of how likely you are to repay what you owe. High scores suggest reliability; low scores raise red flags for lenders.

Key Fact: There is *no* universal credit score. In the UK, the three largest credit reference agencies - **TransUnion**, **Experian**, and **Equifax** - compile your credit file and assign a score using their own formulas. Partner platforms (like **Credit Karma** and **TotallyMoney**) use data from these main agencies, sometimes offering additional services, but fundamentally draw on similar information. As a consequence, you don't know which financial institution will contact which credit bureau. Therefore, you need to check all three to ensure the information they hold on you is correct.

The Building Blocks of Your Credit Score

A healthy credit score and responsible credit card use are about more than numbers - they represent trustworthiness, planning, and control. Staying informed about what affects your score, monitoring your credit report for errors, and cultivating consistent payment habits all add up to better opportunities.

Understanding what influences your score is essential for taking control of your financial future. Here are the factors that matter most:

1. Payment History (35%)

This is the most significant influence on your score. Making consistent, on-time payments for credit cards, loans, and everyday bills demonstrates reliability. Even a single late or missed payment can have a major impact, lowering your score and incurring fees.

2. Credit Utilisation (30%)

Credit utilisation means the proportion of your total credit limits you're currently using. Lenders see high usage (e.g., 'maxing out' your cards) as risky behaviour. As a rule of thumb, keep this figure below 25% - so if your combined limit is £1,000, try to borrow no more than £250 at any time.

3. Length of Credit History (15%)

The longer you have actively and responsibly managed credit, the better for your score. This gives lenders a clear record of your long-term behaviour.

4. New Credit Applications (10%)

Every time you apply for credit, a 'hard' inquiry appears on your report. Too many applications in a short time can indicate financial stress, lowering your score. Hard searches remain visible for about a year.

5. Existing Debt Levels (10%)

Lenders want to know how much you already owe, relative to your income. Excessive debt makes them less likely to extend new credit.

The Impact of Late Payments

A late payment can haunt your credit report for years:

- In the UK, a missed or late payment stays on your file for six years from the date it occurred - regardless of whether you pay the debt later.
- The adverse effect on your score is greatest shortly after the late payment happens, but it lessens as time goes on *if* you continue making payments on time.
- If a late payment appears in error, you can contact the lender or credit bureau to have it corrected. In very rare cases, lenders may remove a late payment as a goodwill gesture if you have a compelling reason (such as a serious illness or an error on their part).

Remember: consistently making payments on time is the best way to repair damage from any accidental slip.

Why Credit Scores Matter

A good credit score can open doors in unexpected ways:

- **Borrowing:** Qualify for loans, credit cards, and mortgages at the lowest interest rates.
- **Renting:** Many landlords check your score to gauge reliability.
- **Employment:** Some employers (e.g., in finance) consider credit history in hiring decisions.
- **Everyday life:** Utility providers and mobile phone companies may run credit checks and offer better terms to those with good scores.

A poor credit score, on the other hand, can lead to denial or higher costs in all these areas.

Remember: setbacks are not permanent. Responsible behaviour today is the foundation for repairing past mistakes and creating a future of financial freedom and choice. Start building these habits now, and you'll reap the rewards for years to come.

Credit Cards: Smart Use, Smart Future

A credit card is often your first and most significant introduction to credit. Used wisely, it can help you build a robust, positive credit history; misused, it can lead to costly mistakes and long-term setbacks.

Best Practices for Credit Card Use

- **Borrow only what you can repay in full each month.** This prevents you from accumulating interest charges, which can be very steep (often 20–30% APR).

- **Pay on time, every time.** Set up reminders or direct debits for at least the minimum payment to never miss a due date.

- **Keep your balance low.** Avoid 'maxing out'- aim to use less than 25% of your limit at any time.

- **Limit new applications.** Only apply for new cards when necessary to avoid unnecessary hard inquiries on your credit score.

Credit Builder Cards

These are cards that can be helpful if you're starting out or rebuilding credit. They often have lower limits and higher interest rates, so use them responsibly.

Pitfalls to Avoid

- **Paying only the minimum:** This causes debt to balloon due to compound interest.

- **Ignoring statements:** Overlooking bills may lead to missed payments and fees.

- **Overusing multiple cards:** Having many unused cards can look risky to lenders; too many active cards can also tempt overspending.

- **Relationship partners:** Be aware that if you're in a relationship or an ex-relationship, your partner's spending habits can impact your credit score.

- **Voter Registration:** If you aren't registered to vote, it makes it difficult for lenders to verify your identity. Getting on the electoral roll helps, but make sure you re-register if or when you move home.

Real Life Example

Lisa, a 30-year-old mother of two, faced credit card debt after being laid off from a full-time job earning about £35,000 a year. With her savings exhausted, she began relying on credit cards to cover daily expenses. As unemployment benefits ran out, Lisa defaulted on her credit card payments. Over time, the high-interest rates and increasing balances made the debt hard to manage. Although she eventually went back to college, found part-time work, and later returned to full-time employment, she is still paying off this credit card debt years later.

Exercises: Build Your Credit Skills

1. Create a Payment Calendar

- Write down all your regular bills and the dates they're due (rent, mortgage, utilities, insurance, credit cards).

- Tick off which payments can be automated - set up direct debits to reduce the risk of forgetting.

2. Budgeting Drill

- Using your total monthly income and fixed expenses, identify how much headroom you have available for discretionary spending and set a personal monthly credit spending limit (ideally, no more than 25% of available credit).

3. Self-Reflection

- Identify financial habits you can implement now to improve your score.

- Consider situations that tend to tempt you to overspend. Brainstorm ahead: What strategies could you use to stay on track, such as leaving credit cards at home during non-essential shopping, or reviewing statements monthly for overspending and errors?

No one wants to waste money. The next chapter offers real-world value, providing practical strategies while remaining grounded in today's digital opportunities for the traditional savvy.

Money-Saving Strategies

5

MONEY-SAVING STRATEGIES

It's crucial to focus on practical tactics that address daily spending in the main areas: food, clothing, household needs, and travel. Maximising limited budgets isn't about relentless sacrifice - it's about making smarter choices, embracing community, and utilising modern tools. With a little planning and a willingness to break free from old shopping habits, you can secure significant savings across the board, sustain your lifestyle, and even help the environment by reducing waste. Every pound you save is a step toward less financial stress and more control.

Introduction: Mindset Matters

As you saw in Chapter 1, your mindset matters. Saving money is as much about mindset as it's about tactics. Approaching purchases with resourcefulness, patience, and a willingness to embrace second-hand, community-based, or alternative options can help dramatically reduce regular expenses. Through a combination of digital platforms and old-fashioned ingenuity, you can maintain a good quality of life on a limited budget.

Food is among the biggest regular expenses, but it also offers significant potential for savings. You can still enjoy good meals and spend less.

Smart Grocery Shopping

Loyalty Schemes: These schemes have surged in popularity as many supermarkets and retailers introduced two-tier pricing, where members pay less for certain products than non-members. An estimated 74% of shoppers hold a Tesco Clubcard, while 50% have a **Nectar** card. Several other schemes, like **Co-op Membership** and **Morrison More, Sainsbury's**, and **Lidl**, offer loyalty cards with digital coupons, points, and personalised discounts, which are also popular.

Yellow Sticker Shopping: You'll usually find a section in all larger supermarkets and some convenience stores with products displaying yellow 'reduced' stickers. These tend to be items that are nearing their best-before or use-by date. Look for markdown sections (often late in the evening) on perishables. Freeze what you can't use immediately.

Bulk Buying & Batch Cooking: Staple foods like rice, pasta, oats, and dried beans are the unsung heroes of budget-friendly eating. When purchased in bulk, think large bags from discount supermarkets or wholesale retailers, the cost per portion drops significantly.

Batch cooking takes this a step further. By prepping meals in advance, say, cooking a big pot of chilli, curry, or pasta bake, you save time during the week and dodge the temptation of pricey takeaways or Deliveroo splurges. It's not just about saving money; it's about reclaiming control over your food choices and eating more healthily.

Grow Your Own and Swap Surplus: Even a windowsill herb garden can save money. Many communities have allotment swaps or '**Freegle**' groups, where gardeners exchange surpluses of homegrown produce. The **Olio** app is another excellent way to find what you need and share what you don't with local people.

Clothing: Style Without the Spend

Clothing budgets can spiral, but with a bit of creativity, you can look sharp without breaking the bank.

Outlet Shopping

An outlet store, factory outlet or factory shop is a brick-and-mortar or online shop where manufacturers sell their merchandise directly to the public. Products at outlet stores are usually sold at reduced prices compared to regular stores because they are overstock, closeout, returned, factory seconds, or lower-quality versions made specifically for outlets.

Charity Shops: A Treasure Trove

UK charity shops (such as **Oxfam**, **British Heart Foundation**, and **Cancer Research UK**) are goldmines for barely worn clothing, shoes, and accessories, including items from top brands.

Swapping and Community Events

Clothes swap events ('swishing parties') are increasingly popular. Swishing is the easy way to update your wardrobe! It's guilt-free shopping with no cost to your wallet and is great for the environment. Swishing works like a giant clothes swap: you bring items you no longer wear and exchange them for something new to you! Check **getswishing.com** and organise your own swap with friends. **Vintage Superstore Kilo** sales are where the organisers bring 9 tonnes of handpicked vintage stock to their events for you to have a rummage through.

Alter and Repair

Simple repairs or alterations (hemming trousers, replacing buttons) can breathe new life into old favourites. **YouTube** offers a wealth of beginner-friendly tutorials, and most towns and cities have an alteration and repair shop. For example, Timpson's is a UK-wide, well-known brand for offering this type of service.

Online Marketplaces

Facebook Marketplace, eBay & Vinted: All are overflowing with new or gently used clothes, often at 10-20% or less of the original price. Filter searches by condition, brand, and location to find bargains nearby.

Depop: Ideal for trendy, vintage, or designer pieces at reduced prices. **Depop** is a circular fashion marketplace where anyone can buy, sell, and discover desirable, affordable second-hand fashion.

Amazon Resale: Whether you're looking for discounts or prefer buying used to extend the life of products, **Amazon Resale** puts returned products back on sale, offering significant savings on a wide selection of quality used, refurbished, or open-box products from your favourite brands.

Household: Furnishing for Less

Household purchases, including furniture, appliances, and décor, can be alarmingly expensive. Here are ways to kit out your home on pennies.

Facebook Marketplace, **Freecycle**, and **Gumtree**. High-quality second-hand items, from sofas to kettles, are often available for a song or even free, as people look to avoid landfill costs. Success depends on timing and haggling: New listings go fast. Set alerts for desired items and politely negotiate on price, especially if you see items relisted after a few days.

Charity Shops and Reuse Centres

Larger charity shops and 'reuse centres' stock furniture and small appliances at a fraction of shop prices. Some even offer delivery for a small fee. Examples include the **British Heart Foundation**, who have charity shops in most town centres, or **Ikea**'s **Re-shop and Re-use** offering.

Repair and Upcycle

Before buying new, see if an appliance or piece of furniture can be repaired. Free workshops and YouTube guides often make minor repairs feasible for novices.

Upcycling, that is, painting, re-covering, or modifying existing items, isn't only a money-saving endeavour but also a rewarding one.

Travel: Getting from A to B, Affordably

Personal transportation is costly, but there are several ways to reduce travel expenses.

Public Transport Hacks

Railcards: If eligible (16-25, disabled, family & friends), **UK Railcards** offer up to 33% off train fares.

Advance and Split Ticketing: Book tickets in advance and use apps that 'split' tickets (buying segments separately) for a lower overall price.

Carpooling and Sharing

BlaBlaCar: Connects drivers with spare seats to passengers heading in the same direction, at a much cheaper rate than the train. The UK's largest carpooling network now offers affordable coach travel across Europe.

Liftshare and **Car Clubs**: are great for daily commutes or occasional trips; car clubs like **Zipcar** let you rent by the hour.

Cycling and Walking

For short local trips, invest in a good bike (buy used from local sources), or take advantage of the growing number of UK bike-sharing schemes.

General Tips and Tech Apps

Plan Before You Shop: Make lists and avoid impulse purchasing. Consider a 'cooling-off' period for non-essential items.

Borrow, Don't Buy: Libraries lend more than books these days; tools, toys, and even kitchen equipment. So, try borrowing rather than buying from the **Library of Things**.

The Modern Saver's Toolkit

- **Leverage technology** for the best prices and cashback opportunities.
- **Comparison Sites:** For utilities, insurance, and monthly bills, use sites like **MoneySuperMarket** or **Uswitch** to secure the best deals.
- **Cashback Programs:** Apps like **Quidco** and **TopCashback** refund you a percentage of what you spend at participating retailers, both online and in-store.
- **Voucher Apps: Honey**, **VoucherCodes**, and **supermarket apps** often instantly apply discounts and codes to your online basket.
- **Loyalty Cards:** Many retailers provide discounts through loyalty cards. If you frequently visit a specific coffee shop or retail store, you can use the loyalty card to receive free or discounted products.

> Exercises:
>
> Reflect on your spending for one month
>
> - At the end of the month, from your records, categorise your spending (food, travel, social, study materials, etc.) if you've not already done so.
> - Highlight any purchase you realise was an impulse buy or could have been replaced with a cheaper alternative.
>
> Research Saving Opportunities for yourself in your area for these categories:
>
> - Food and general shopping
> - Regular Bills
> - Travel
> - Discounts available
>
> Challenge
>
> - No-Spend Day: Designate one day when you spend nothing on non-essentials. Note what you do differently to succeed.

The next chapter stresses increasing your income while being careful with your spending. You will discover that building wealth isn't just about reducing expenses. You should aim to boost your income and manage your spending wisely.

Building Your Financial Future

6

BUILDING YOUR FINANCIAL FUTURE

Building Wealth: It's Not Just About Cutting Back

To truly build wealth, you need to focus on *increasing your income* as well as being smart with spending. Think beyond saving leftovers from your student loan or job - consider ways to boost your earnings and make your money grow on its own. This could mean starting a side hustle, developing high-demand skills, or getting savvy about investing early. Over time, these choices can open doors - like affording a flat, taking more freedom with your career, or travelling without stress about money.

What's Holding You Back from Investing?

Many young people assume that *investing* is just for City types or the super-rich, but that's outdated thinking. Even a small amount, say £25 a month, can get you started, as previously mentioned. The earlier you start, the more you benefit from compound interest: that's where your money earns profits, and those profits start earning profits too, growing faster over the years. Waiting until you 'feel ready' or have 'spare' money can cost you years of growth, making long-term goals like buying a home or enjoying a work break harder to achieve.

Example:
If you start investing at age 22, just £30 a month at 6% annual growth could become over £20,000 by your mid-40s, without doing anything fancy.

Robo-Advisors: Smart Tech for Beginners

Robo-advisors are like a Pocket Spotify for your investments. They're apps or online services that design and manage your investment portfolio automatically. Here's how it works:

- You answer simple questions: Your age, income, what you're saving for (like a house deposit or gap year), how much risk you're okay with, and how long you plan to invest.

- The robo-advisor builds a diversified portfolio, e.g., 70% stocks (riskier, but long-term growth) and 30% bonds (more stable).

- It *automatically* balances your investments as markets change or as you approach your goal - literally set-and-forget.

- Fees are much lower than speaking to a traditional financial advisor, and the apps are often designed to be friendly and jargon-free.

For Gen Z, some popular options are **Nutmeg**, **Moneybox**, or **Wealthify**. Make sure any service you use is authorised by the FCA (Financial Conduct Authority) to keep your money safe.

Understanding Leverage – with Caution

Leverage refers to using borrowed money to increase your returns on investment, whether in property, business, or financial markets.

An Example of How Leverage Works

If you have £1,000 and borrow another £1,000, you can invest £2,000. If your investment grows by 10%, you profit by £200; however, you owe interest on the borrowed amount and must repay it regardless of any gains or losses.

Used well, leverage can amplify profits and help you access opportunities you couldn't otherwise afford. Mortgages are a typical example of leverage in everyday use. In the world of UK property investing and buy-to-let investing, leverage refers to the practice of using borrowed funds, most commonly through a buy-to-let mortgage, to finance the purchase of a property. Instead of paying the full price of the property upfront, you, as an investor, contribute a deposit (often ranging from 20% to 40% of the property's value) and borrow the remainder from a lender. This approach allows you to control a high-value asset with a relatively small amount of your own capital, magnifying both potential returns and potential risks

Used poorly, leverage can magnify losses and quickly lead to financial distress.

Real Life Example

A few years ago, Josh decided to try his hand at investing in stocks, hoping to grow his savings faster. He had read online forums about 'margin accounts,' which allow you to borrow money from your broker to buy more shares than you could with just your own cash. The idea of doubling his buying power was exciting, so he signed up.

Initially, the market was rising, and his portfolio grew faster than he'd ever seen. He felt clever and confident. But then, unexpectedly, a company in his portfolio reported disappointing earnings, and the market fell. Because he was leveraged, meaning he'd borrowed money to invest, his losses weren't just his own: he owed significantly more than he'd invested.

His broker called with a 'margin call,' demanding he deposit more cash to cover the losses. This forced him to sell some investments at a loss just to meet the requirement. He realised that leverage had turned a manageable loss into a cost he couldn't easily recover from. For months afterwards, he struggled to rebuild his savings, wishing he'd been content to invest only what he actually had.

Ignoring Tax Savings or Side Income Potential

- **Compound Interest:** As said earlier, think of compound interest as 'free money over time.' When you invest, you earn returns - and next year, you earn on both your original investment and those returns. The longer you invest, the bigger the snowball effect. Most people regret not starting sooner!

- **Tax Savings:** In the UK, you can grow your investments tax-free with products like a **Stocks and Shares ISA**. You don't pay UK tax on money you make inside these accounts, up to an annual limit (currently £20,000). That means more of your money stays yours.

- **Side Hustles:** Don't underestimate small gigs! Selling old clothes on **Depop**, tutoring, or building social media content can start as pocket money but grow into real income streams. Anything you earn, after expenses, can be invested for the future.

Combining a side hustle *and* investing the extra cash, even in small amounts, can move your wealth journey along faster than you think.

Investing for Your Future: Stocks, Bonds, Crypto, and Crowdfunding

Investing has often seemed beyond reach for those without high incomes or family wealth, yet today, there are more ways than ever for Gen Z in the UK to start, even with modest sums. Stocks represent partial ownership in companies listed on exchanges like the **London Stock Exchange**; buying shares means you benefit if the company does well, but you also risk your money if it falters. Bonds are essentially IOUs - you lend money to a company or government in exchange for interest over time. They tend to be less risky than stocks but provide smaller returns.

Cryptocurrencies, such as **Bitcoin** and **Ethereum**, are digital currencies that operate independently of central bank control. Although their prices can fluctuate sharply, they are highly volatile and less heavily regulated than stocks and bonds.

Crowdfunding through platforms like **GoFundMe** or **Crowdcube** allows you to invest small amounts to support start-ups, often in exchange for shares. However, these ventures carry risks, with many new businesses failing.

These assets might seem complex, but their core is straightforward: the chance to grow your money over time, each carrying different levels of risk and reward. The key is to learn the fundamentals, understand what you're investing in, and never invest more than you can afford to lose.

Accessible platforms such as **Freetrade**, **Trading212**, or even some banking apps, allow you to buy 'fractional' shares, so you're not excluded from investing in large firms due to high share prices. Index funds and 'robo-advisors' offer ready-made, diversified baskets for beginners. The market will fluctuate, but over the course of decades, consistent, modest investing in funds that track the overall market generally outperforms trying to 'pick winners.'

Avoiding Scams and 'Get Rich Quick' Traps

With the rise of online investing and cryptocurrencies, scams aimed at young and inexperienced investors have increased. 'Pump and dump' crypto schemes, fake trading platforms, and guaranteed returns are common and even promoted by influencers. In the UK, investment firms must be authorised by the FCA

(Financial Conduct Authority); always verify their registration before investing.

A simple rule: if something sounds too good to be true, like guaranteed profits or secret investing tricks, it almost certainly is. Genuine investing focuses on long-term growth, not instant wealth. Protect yourself by researching, using reputable platforms, and consulting experienced investors or trusted sources before making decisions.

Real Life Examples
Example 1: A First-Time Investor's Journey

Ethan, aged 20 from Liverpool, wanted to make his savings work harder. He started with £10 a month into a stocks and shares ISA through a popular app. By reading up on index funds, he realised he didn't need to pick individual stocks but could invest in the FTSE 100, owning a small stake in the UK's largest companies. Year by year, he saw his account fluctuate - but over time, his balance trended upwards, giving him confidence and a practical lesson in staying calm during market ups and downs.

Example 2: Avoiding Crypto Scams

Jade, a graphic design apprentice in Glasgow, was tempted by crypto after seeing 'success stories' on TikTok. She nearly fell for a trading group that promised big monthly returns for a hefty membership fee. Double-checking with the FCA register, she found the firm wasn't authorised. Instead, she joined a free online community for young investors. She learned the basics safely, eventually dabbling with £50 in legitimate cryptocurrency exchanges, although aware that it was a high-risk punt and not a certainty.

Exercise: Your Wealth-Building Journey

1. **Choose to Start Investing or Start a Side Hustle**
   - Research a beginner-friendly robo-advisor (e.g., Nutmeg, Moneybox) or other low-fee investment platform authorised in the UK.
   - Or, brainstorm three side hustles you could realistically start this month. List the steps and what skills you'd need.

2. **Find Your ISA**
   - Google 'Best Stocks & Shares ISA UK Gen Z' and pick one top-rated option to review. Note the fees charged, the minimum deposit amount, and whether they offer app-based features for beginners.

3. **Scam Spotting Considerations**

   - For each statement, mark: SAFE or RED FLAG. After answering, review any 'guaranteed' claims, pressure tactics, or missing company information. Always check the FCA register or visit the Companies House website.

   - The platform is registered with the FCA and clearly explains investment risks.

   - You're promised a 'guaranteed return' of 20% within one month.

   - The website features influencer testimonials but no physical business address.

   - You can only pay in via cryptocurrency.

4. **Starter Investment Plan**
   - Using an app or website, research & list five FTSE 100 companies, a UK government bond ('gilt'), & one global index fund.
   - Set a goal to invest even £10 per month, choose one that fits your values and tolerance for risk.
   - Write down your personal 'investment rules' (e.g., only invest money not needed for living expenses, maintain a sanity check of your financial situation, review your plan at least annually).

> **5. Peer Accountability**
> - Join a beginner investing group (in person or online, e.g., The MoneySavingExpert forums or Reddit's UKPersonalFinance).
> - Share your plan with a colleague or group, track your progress monthly, and discuss emotional responses to news or market fluctuations.

This new world demands lifelong learning. The shift from education to employment is undergoing significant upheavals. The next chapter will guide you through your options, outlining the pros and cons of various approaches.

From College to Apprenticeships to Self-Taught

7

FROM COLLEGE TO APPRENTICESHIPS TO SELF-TAUGHT

The Pros & Cons of University, Apprenticeships, Gap Years, and Self-Learning

Navigating the path from education to a rewarding career is becoming more diverse in the UK. The idea of university as the 'default' route is being challenged as young people consider alternatives, such as apprenticeships, gap years, and self-taught skills gained through online resources.

University degrees confer social status and can open doors to certain professions such as medicine and law. However, tuition fees are high, and securing graduate jobs isn't guaranteed. Many Gen Z students graduate with substantial student loans. The repayment system in the UK adjusts payments based on income, easing the burden, but the costs and competition for jobs remain significant.

Apprenticeships, offered in areas from engineering to digital marketing, combine earning with learning. They are paid, typically debt-free, and help towards a smooth move into the workforce. Some include university-level study, known as 'higher apprenticeships' or 'degree apprenticeships,' allowing you to earn a degree while working.

A well-organised gap year isn't a 'waste of time.' It can foster maturity, broaden experiences, or develop skills - through travel, volunteering, or paid employment. Meanwhile, the growth of self-taught careers is driven by resources like YouTube, Coursera, and coding bootcamps. Employers are increasingly valuing portfolios and demonstrable skills over formal qualifications, particularly in the tech, design, or creative industries.

The key is to research your field and your preferences; the right path strikes a balance between financial realities, learning style, and future goals.

Building a Portfolio & Networking in the Digital Age

Regardless of your path, creating a portfolio, your collection of work, skills, or contributions, is becoming increasingly vital. For creative industries, platforms like **Behance**, **GitHub**, or personal websites display projects and talents. Even outside arts or technology, evidence of volunteering, part-time roles, or independent initiatives can set you apart from others.

Networking is no longer confined to formal events. Youth today find mentors and connections through platforms like **LinkedIn, Discord servers, X (Twitter)**, and dedicated communities such as **YRDS** or the **King's Trust** (formerly Prince's Trust). Reaching out for virtual coffee chats, attending webinars, or participating in hackathons can create opportunities that traditional education no longer provides. The ability to present yourself online and engage with supportive communities is now as vital as having a polished CV.

Real Life Example
Example 1

In the UK, stories of self-made YouTubers, coders, artists, or activists inspire a re-evaluation of what success 'should' look like. Take Alice, a self-taught programmer from Newcastle who developed mobile apps and contributed to open-source projects on GitHub. Without a computer science degree, she secured a position at a tech firm after gaining recognition on an online coding forum. Or Marcus, who took a gap year to volunteer with a mental health charity, discovered a passion for advocacy, and now works in social enterprise - demonstrating that following curiosity, rather than just gathering credentials, can lead to fulfilling careers.

These paths demonstrate that resilience, adaptability, and initiative are often more valuable than a single impressive qualification.

Example 2: Self-Taught Designer

Emma, 19, from Brighton, learned graphic design through online tutorials and started freelancing for local businesses during the pandemic. Her digital portfolio attracted clients and resulted in a remote job offer with a London creative agency, demonstrating that skill and persistence can outweigh traditional routes.

Exercises

1. Career Path Mapping Exercise

- Draw a flowchart or mind-map using an app like VisualMind, of at least three possible career routes: e.g., university, apprenticeship, self-taught, change of career, etc.
- List the requirements, costs, benefits, pitfalls, and possible first steps for each.
- Research typical starting salaries or increases in salary, time to qualify, and examples of people who followed each path.

2. Portfolio Starter Kit

- Choose a platform like LinkedIn, a personal website, or GitHub, and outline what to showcase: projects, certificates, work samples, or volunteering.
- Upload your first project, CV, or post about your learning journey.
- Set a monthly reminder to add new experiences or skills.

3. Digital Networking Challenge

- Join a relevant online community (LinkedIn group, industry forum, Discord server).
- Reach out to someone in a career you're interested in - ask for advice or insight into how they started.
- Attend one virtual event or webinar and write down three takeaways or contacts.

The gig economy has arrived. The world of work is undergoing significant changes; career paths are no longer linear, and AI & robotics are becoming more widespread. The next chapter examines your options, highlighting the advantages and disadvantages of various approaches.

Earning in the Age of AI: Jobs, Gigs, & Side Hustles

8

EARNING IN THE AGE OF AI: JOBS, GIGS, & SIDE HUSTLES

The Gig Economy: Opportunities and Pitfalls

The UK work landscape has undergone a significant transformation for Gen Z, with the traditional concept of a 'job for life' giving way to multiple income streams and flexible, on-demand gig work. Platforms like **Deliveroo**, **Uber**, **TaskRabbit**, and digital marketplaces such as **Depop** or **Fiverr** make it simple to pick up work as needed. The appeal is obvious: set your own hours, work from anywhere, and monetise skills from driving to digital design.

However, the reality is more complicated. Gig work often lacks employment protections, including paid holidays, pensions, and job security. Income can be unpredictable, and competition is fierce, especially online. Furthermore, HMRC considers earnings over £1,000 per year from side hustles as taxable income; maintaining detailed records and submitting self-assessment tax returns is essential.

For some, gigs provide a route to independence; for others, they involve managing instability with the dream of 'making it.' Recognising both perspectives is crucial for making well-informed decisions.

Ways of Working

Getting a job and turning up at some building for work is no longer the norm. The move is towards remote working, freelancing, contracting, or being a digital nomad. Here's how they interrelate and the implications in today's global workforce.

1. Remote workers are individuals who perform their job duties outside their company's physical office. Their roles can be either as employees or contractors, and they usually work from home, coworking spaces, cafés, or even while travelling. The pandemic hastened the shift towards remote work, removing geographical limitations and making it practical for both companies and talent. The main advantage is flexibility; remote workers enjoy the freedom to select their work environment, often needing only a laptop and an internet connection. A remote worker can also overlap with the digital nomad identity if they work away from their home or company base for long periods.

2. Freelancers and Contractors are independent professionals who do not have traditional employment relationships with a single company. While contractors might work exclusively with one client, freelancers tend to juggle multiple clients and projects, often on a short-term or ongoing basis. Both are self-employed and have control over their workload and schedules; however, establishing consistent client relationships and a stable income can be challenging. Freelancers and contractors can also be digital nomads if they choose to work in locations far from their clients. Contractors may fall under the remote worker category if their role is similar to an employed position, but without benefits such as healthcare or paid leave.

3. Digital Nomads are defined more by lifestyle than work arrangement. They travel the world, working online from various countries, typically on tourist visas that usually allow for short stays. The digital nomad lifestyle offers adventure and freedom but is less stable, often lacking permanence and routine. Digital nomads can be remote workers, freelancers, or contractors; what distinguishes them is their mobility and the fact that their work allows for continuous travel. In recent years, many countries (such as Portugal, Croatia, and Estonia) have introduced special visas permitting digital nomads to live and work within their borders beyond regular tourist limits, highlighting the growing appeal and legitimacy of this modern working style.

In essence, these ways of working describe the evolving nature of work in a post-pandemic world, where technology enables flexible, location-independent careers. Understanding their differences and overlaps will help you decide which path aligns best with your aspirations, be they remote employment stability, freelance autonomy, or the adventurous digital nomad lifestyle.

How AI & Automation Are Changing Traditional Jobs

Artificial intelligence and automation are rapidly transforming the UK workforce. The current form of AI essentially functions as brain augmentation, increasing your capacity to perform tasks, often digital in nature, such as enhanced writing skills, creative design, music, image manipulation, and coding. The next generation of AI tools will have a more significant impact on employment, the economy, society, and government. Jobs in manufacturing, administration, and even professional fields like law and finance are changing as routine tasks become automated. For Gen Z, this brings new challenges but also new opportunities:

the demand for digital skills, creative thinking, and adaptability is growing.

Careers in data analysis, programming, content creation, and green technologies are growing, while soft skills like communication and problem-solving remain highly valued. Instead of fearing AI, viewing it as a tool, one that can enhance work or free up time for innovation, gives Gen Z an edge. Upskilling through online courses, apprenticeships, or tech bootcamps now equals the value of a traditional university degree.

Entrepreneurial Mindsets: Turning Passions into Income Streams

For many young people, side hustles are more than just financial stopgaps; they are a means to achieve personal growth and financial stability. They serve as a path to personal expression and entrepreneurship. Whether it's starting a **YouTube** channel about coding, selling handmade jewellery on **Etsy**, or tutoring GCSE students online, the barriers to entry are lower than ever. Social media enables quick brand-building and direct access to potential customers.

However, entrepreneurial life isn't just about the 'be your own boss' glamour. Many Gen Zers experience burnout, face inconsistent pay, or need to learn the basics of administration and legal matters (such as registering as self-employed and tracking expenses). Nevertheless, perseverance pays off: small ventures can develop into full-time businesses or transform hobbies into sustainable supplementary income, sometimes offering flexibility and fulfilment that traditional jobs often lack.

How to Spot Opportunities and Take Action

1. Develop an Opportunity Mindset

The first step in spotting opportunities is to actively look for them. Opportunities arise from a willingness to observe, listen, and keep an open mind, as chances are often present, but you need to be primed to spot them.

Cultivate curiosity: ask, "What could be better here?" or, "What does my community or industry need that is currently missing?" Thinking this way creates space for innovative ideas.

2. Leverage Your Digital Edge

Gen Z excels at using technology to research, connect, and explore new paths. Use social media, online forums, and professional networking sites to:

- Identify emerging trends.
- Follow inspiring people or organisations.
- Get real, crowd-sourced insights about issues, solutions, and gaps others have spotted.
- Participate in online communities: sometimes opportunities are shared or discovered in these digital spaces.

3. Identify Problems as Opportunities

Every problem can be transformed into a potential opportunity. Identify pain points in your environment, school, workplace, or community. If something is frustrating, inefficient, or unfair, is there a way to address or enhance it?

Utilise frameworks like the SWOT analysis (Strengths, Weaknesses, Opportunities, and Threats) to systematically identify gaps that can be filled or strengths that can be leveraged.

4. Take Action: Move from Idea to Execution

Gather knowledge: Read, research, and learn rapidly about the area or problem you've spotted. This helps you understand context and builds confidence to act.

Don't wait for a perfect plan; take small, practical steps toward testing your idea or solution. Prototyping, volunteering for new projects, or starting side hustles all count.

Make contacts, as opportunities are often linked to the people you know. Build networks, attend events (virtual or in-person), and reach out to others with similar goals for collaboration and support.

5. Embrace Feedback and Continuous Learning

Ask for feedback early and often. Reflecting on what's working (and what isn't) will help you refine your action and pivot when necessary.

Remember: Most opportunities come from a willingness to stretch out of your comfort zone and learn as you go.

6. Align Opportunities with Your Values

Gen Zers are particularly motivated by purpose and ethical alignment. Spotting the right opportunity isn't just about what's profitable; it's about what matches your personal values, ambitions, and sense of impact.

Filter possible opportunities through questions like:

- Does this reflect what's important to me?
- Will it help others or solve a real need?
- Is this an environment (or community) where I can grow?

Quick Checklist for Gen Zers:

- Spot the gaps. Every time you hit a roadblock or get frustrated, ask: *"How could this be better?"* That's your cue for innovation.
- Leverage your digital edge. Utilise your online skills to research quickly, join communities, and connect with people across borders.
- Flip problems into projects. Break down challenges using simple analysis tools to uncover where the real opportunity lies.
- Move, even if it's small. Big wins often start with tiny first steps; just make that first move.
- Grow your circle, like developer and coding communities, join the **Discord** server that allows you to interact through text, voice, and video, and connect with people who think differently from you, and don't be afraid to ask for ideas and feedback.
- Stay true to your values. Focus on opportunities that align with your beliefs and the kind of future you want to shape.

By applying this approach, Gen Zers can confidently spot and seize opportunities - whether for entrepreneurial ventures, career advances, or meaningful projects - in today's fast-changing world.

Creating Multiple Income Streams

Building multiple income streams requires effort, but finding and evaluating the right opportunities is achievable with a structured approach. You can identify genuine opportunities, weigh effort against reward, and view practical examples.

1. How to Find Income Stream Opportunities

Start with your skills and interests: Your professional expertise, hobbies, or assets all have value. For example, consulting, coaching, or selling digital products based on your know-how can be easier and more rewarding than starting from scratch in an unfamiliar area.

Look for low-barrier-to-entry options: Many income streams need little upfront cash but do require time or skills (e.g., freelancing, online courses, affiliate marketing, renting out spare assets like a spare room).

Monitor current trends: Follow online communities, social media, or industry publications. Changes in technology, remote work, or consumer habits often present new gaps for you to fill, especially in digital products or services.

2. Evaluating Reward vs Effort

Ask yourself:

- How much upfront effort or skill is needed? (e.g., setting up a drop-shipping store vs. Freelance writing).

- Is it mostly active (trading your time) or can it become passive (earning while you sleep)?

- What's the likely return? Consider your target monthly goal. However, don't forget that some streams may take months to show significant returns.

- Does it fit your lifestyle and schedule? Be realistic about available hours, willingness to learn, and what tasks you enjoy (or hate) doing.

- Is it scalable? Some ideas, such as digital products, can grow with minimal extra effort after launch, while others, like gig work, require ongoing hours to earn more.

Typically, streams with higher passive potential (e.g., dividends, digital products, rental property) require more initial effort or capital but less ongoing work. Purely active options, such as dog walking or freelancing, are easier to start, but they involve trading your time directly for money.

Tips to Succeed

- Start small, test, and iterate: Try simple or low-cost streams first and scale up as you learn what works.

- Be selective: Say no to low-reward, high-effort ideas. Focus on what plays to your strengths and fits your time budget.

- Automate where possible: Utilise technology to minimise manual involvement (e.g., scheduling posts, automating e-commerce processes).

- Keep learning and pivoting: The most resilient income strategies involve adapting to shifts in demand, technology, or your own interests.

- Diversifying your income is possible even with limited resources, provided you're realistic about effort, choose wisely, and learn as you go. The key: start, tweak, and let compounding effort - and results - work in your favour.

Real Life Examples

Example 1: Digital Side Hustle for University Fees

Sophie, a psychology student in Bristol, began offering resumé editing as a side gig through Fiverr. Initially earning just £5 per job, she built up a portfolio and received glowing reviews. By her second year, Sophie's side hustle had paid for her textbooks and part of her rent, all while providing her with valuable insights into careers and networking opportunities with professionals globally.

Example 2: Adapting to Automation

Raj, aged 22, in Leicester, lost a part-time admin job as his employer switched to automated systems. Instead of panicking, Raj completed a free online course in digital marketing. Within months, he was using AI tools to manage small business social media campaigns, earning more than before, and finding a new career direction.

Exercises
1. Side Hustle Brainstorm Worksheet
- List five things you're good at or enjoy (e.g., video editing, baking, fitness coaching).
- For each, think of one way you could earn money (e.g., YouTube tutorials, selling cakes at local markets, offering virtual classes).

- Research whether you could do it online or locally, what basic equipment or monetary investment you'd need & potential profits.

2. Risk Assessment and Planning
- For your top two side hustle ideas, list the pros (flexibility, control, learning) and potential cons (irregular income, start-up costs, time needed).
- Identify at least three challenges for each, e.g. such as setting prices, dealing with customers, or balancing work & study, & suggest solutions.
- Identify at least two online communities (like Reddit's UKPersonalFinance or LinkedIn groups) where you could get support from others with similar goals.

3. Self-Employment Basics
- Research HMRC's 'trading allowance' and what it means for side income. Write down what steps you'd need to register as self-employed in the UK and what records to keep.

Life is unpredictable, even for young adults. The next chapter covers protecting your wealth, what makes you vulnerable, and the role of insurance and emergency funds.

are too important to leave it for granted until
The next chapter covers protecting your
wealth; what makes you vulnerable, and the
roles of insurance and emergency funds.

Protecting Your Wealth

9

PROTECTING YOUR WEALTH

Protect Your Wealth: Insurance & Emergency Funds

1. What Leaves You Vulnerable: Life is unpredictable, even for young adults with steady income or student loans. If you don't have an emergency fund, unexpected events can hit hard. For example, your phone could break, your car might fail its MOT, or you could face sudden unemployment or medical issues. Without a cash buffer, you may be forced to use high-interest credit cards or payday loans, which can quickly lead to long-term debt and financial stress. Having a dedicated emergency fund, typically three to six months' worth of living expenses, ensures you can cover these surprises without derailing your future plans.

2. Underestimating Insurance: Insurance is about protecting what's important and safeguarding your future. Many young people assume insurance is for later, but in the UK, even a minor accident can create significant financial issues if you're uninsured. For example:

- **Home or renters' insurance:** Essential for anyone renting or owning property, protecting possessions from theft, fire, or flooding; a real risk with increasing extreme weather events in the UK.

- **Health insurance:** While the NHS covers most needs, private health insurance can help you avoid long waiting lists and cover services not provided by the NHS, especially dental or vision care.

- **Gadget insurance:** With smartphones and laptops vital for work and study, protecting them against theft or accidental damage can save headaches and expense. Ignoring insurance risks your savings, credit rating, and opportunities if things go wrong may be at risk.

- **Freelancers** and the self-employed need robust health or income protection insurance, since they have no employer sick pay or benefits to fall back on.

- **Frequent travellers, digital nomads,** or students studying abroad should consider travel insurance for health, lost luggage, or cancellations.

3. Relying on Luck Instead of Planning: It's tempting to think, "Nothing bad will happen to me," but relying on luck leaves you exposed. Proactive planning, setting aside an emergency fund and having the right insurance give you control over your financial security. It means you don't have to rely on a last-minute loan, move back in with family, or interrupt your studies or career. Planning is empowerment, not pessimism.

Real Life Example:

If your laptop is essential for university or remote working, gadget insurance can provide a replacement quickly if it's lost or stolen, so you don't miss deadlines or a pay cheque. In contrast, without coverage, replacing a vital device could eat up your emergency savings or push you into debt.

Exercise: Build Your Personal Safety Net

1. **Calculate Your Emergency Fund:**
   - List your essential monthly expenses (rent, food, transport, mobile bill).
   - Multiply by three. This is your minimum emergency fund goal.

- How much do you already have saved? Set a date to reach your goal.

2. **Insurance Checklist**
   - Are you covered for home/contents, health, travel, and gadgets?
   - What would you lose if something important were stolen, lost, or damaged?
   - Choose one area where you feel most vulnerable. Research insurance options available. Look for student deals, joint policies, or age-specific discounts.

3. **Discussion Prompt:**
   - Reflect or share with a friend: What's the most unexpected expense you've faced, and how did you handle it, or how could you handle it better next time?

Three things are certain in this life: change, taxes, & death. But taxes are present in every aspect of your life, spending, saving, earning & dying. The next chapter covers the basics of the UK Tax system & how you can legally minimise your liability.

The UK Tax System Basics

10

THE UK TAX SYSTEM BASICS

Basics of the UK Tax System (2025)

There are three certainties in life: change, death and taxes. Here, we focus on taxes since you will be liable for them sooner rather than later, and it's useful to understand them. The most common taxes are income tax and Value Added Tax (VAT), the latter of which you will have already been paying, but might be unaware of.

Income Tax: Most people pay income tax on their earnings, which include their salary, side-hustle income, self-employment income, savings interest, dividends, rental profits, and pension income. However, you're allowed to earn £12,570 without paying any tax. This is your Personal Tax Allowance, meaning that the first £12,570 of your annual income is tax-free. It used to increase annually in line with inflation, but since March 2021, it has been frozen at the current rate, though it's set to rise again in April

2028. Beyond that, everything you earn is subject to taxation, but the amount isn't the same across all earnings and is banded, meaning the more you earn, the greater your income tax liability.

Tax Bands 2025:

- £12,571–£50,270 at 20% (basic rate)
- £50,271–£125,140 at 40% (higher rate)
- Over £125,140 at 45% (additional rate)
- If your income is over £100,000, your personal allowance decreases by £1 for every £2 you earn above this threshold.

Along with Income Tax, you will also be liable for National Insurance (NI): Employees and the self-employed contribute to NI, which funds benefits and the state pension. The rate and rules depend on your type of work and earnings.

- In 2025, employees pay up to 8%, and employers contribute up to 15%.

Other Taxes: UK residents also pay VAT, Value Added Tax (on goods/services), council tax (local services), capital gains tax (profits from selling assets), and sometimes inheritance tax or stamp duty.

Ways to Legally Reduce UK Taxes

1. Use Your Personal Allowance: Make sure all your income is accounted for to use the full £12,570 personal allowance before paying income tax.

2. Benefit from ISA Accounts: Invest in ISAs (Individual Savings Accounts): Interest, dividends, and capital gains made in an ISA are tax-free. There is an annual ISA allowance cap (£20,000 in 2025).

3. Contribute to Your Pension: Pension contributions are tax-deductible and can reduce your taxable income. Your employer also must contribute to your workplace pension if you're employed, boosting your retirement pot and reducing tax liability.

4. Claim Work-Related Expenses: If you're self-employed or have a side-hustle, you can offset allowable business expenses against your taxable income, such as website costs, equipment, and travel directly related to your business.

If you earn less than £3,000 of side-hustle income, you may not need to file a tax return due to new thresholds in 2025.

5. Take Advantage of Other Allowances: Dividend Allowance: First £500 of dividend income is tax-free (2025/26). Savings Allowance: Basic rate taxpayers can earn up to £1,000 interest on savings tax-free.

6. Gift Aid Contributions: If you donate to charity through **Gift Aid**, charities claim an extra 25% and you can claim extra tax relief if you pay higher or additional rate tax.

7. Use the Marriage Allowance (if eligible): If married or in a civil partnership and one partner is a non-taxpayer, some of their unused allowance can be transferred to the other.

8. Side-Hustle and Online Sales: You need to declare income if selling online or gig working, but only if you exceed the reporting threshold (£3,000 from 2025). Stay under this threshold, if possible, to avoid extra paperwork.

9. Plan for Student Loan Repayments: For Gen Z, student loan repayments act effectively as an extra tax. Prioritise financial planning to manage high effective tax rates when crossing certain income bands.

Key Takeaways

- Always maintain precise records of your income, side-hustles, and expenses, especially if you have more than one source of earnings.

- File tax returns promptly if required and claim every allowance and relief you're eligible for.

- Start early with pensions and ISAs: The earlier you start, the more you benefit from tax-free growth and employer contributions.

- Use HMRC's resources (and free guidance) to check eligibility for specific allowances or reliefs.

- With some planning and awareness of your entitlement, you can make sure you only pay what you owe - and put more money into your own future.

Real Life Example

Jane, a UK employee earning £45,000 a year, regularly pays income tax at 20% on her earnings above the personal allowance (£12,570). After learning about the UK tax system basics, she decided to maximise tax efficiency legally.

- ***Personal Allowance:*** *Jane ensured she fully benefited from her personal allowance, which meant her first £12,570 of income was tax-free.*
- ***Pension Contributions:*** *She increased her pension contributions. Because pension payments are made before tax, this reduced her taxable income, effectively lowering the amount subject to the 20% income tax rate.*
- ***ISA Account:*** *Jane also contributed the maximum allowed to an Individual Savings*

Account (ISA), where interest and dividends are tax-free.

By utilising personal allowances, tax-efficient savings such as ISAs, and pension contributions, Jane effectively reduced her taxable income, paid less income tax, and increased her savings, all within the UK tax rules.

Exercises

1. **Review Your Income and Savings**

   - Make a note of your primary sources of income (salary, self-employment, interest, dividends, etc

   - Identify the **2025/26 Personal Allowance** (£12,570) and ensure you know how much of your income is tax-free.

2. **Apply your Allowances**

   - Check if you're using tax-free accounts: *Are you maximising contributions to ISAs? Are you contributing to a pension?*

3. **Explore Legal Tax Reduction Strategies**

   - Have you asked your employer about **salary sacrifice schemes** (e.g., pension contributions, childcare vouchers)?

- Are you claiming all possible reliefs (such as marriage allowance, disability allowance, or work-related expenses)?

- Do you have any income that could be shifted to a lower-taxed spouse (if married/civil partnered)?

- Could you increase pension or charitable contributions to reduce taxable income further?

4. **Create a Tax-Smart Action Plan**

    - Note two practical steps to take in the next month that will make your situation more tax-efficient.

    - Commit to revisiting your plan annually, ideally before the end of the tax year.

Negotiations involve finding a solution acceptable to all parties. Mastering effective negotiation is an important skill. The next chapter examines negotiating from a value-based perspective, emphasising core principles and strategies.

Negotiation & Value-Based Thinking

11

NEGOTIATION & VALUE-BASED THINKING

What Is Negotiation, & Why It Matters to Gen Z?

Negotiation is the process of reaching a solution that is acceptable to all parties involved, who may have different aims or interests. For Gen Zers, negotiation goes beyond merely bargaining for a higher salary or a better deal; it involves understanding your worth, confidently standing up for yourself, and making sure that agreements reflect your values and sense of purpose.

Gen Z is increasingly reshaping negotiation to focus on authenticity, fairness, and values. Rather than viewing negotiation as a win-lose or purely transactional process, many Gen Zers approach it as a means to align decisions with their principles on matters such as inclusion, sustainability, well-being, and equity.

Value-Based Thinking in Negotiation

Value-based thinking is an approach that identifies what matters most to both parties, aiming to create solutions that deliver long-term benefits, not just quick wins. This contrasts with traditional methods, which focus mainly on 'who gets what.' Instead, Gen Zers are more likely to:

- Seek outcomes aligned with their values and goals.
- Want agreements to reflect fairness and mutual benefit.
- Consider the broader impact of their choices, not just immediate personal gain.
- Be prepared to walk away from deals that don't fit their ethical or lifestyle standard.

Core Principles and Strategies

Principled Negotiation: Focuses on four key steps:

1. Separate people from the problem: distinguish emotional issues from the main topics to communicate clearly and constructively.
2. Focus on interests, not fixed positions: ask "why do I (or they) want this?" which uncovers true needs, leading to creative and satisfying outcomes.

3. Invent options for mutual gain: brainstorm solutions that give both sides as much value as possible.
4. Use objective criteria: base agreements on fair, transparent standards.

Values-Based Negotiation: Requires self-awareness (knowing what you believe in) as well as skills like active listening, empathy, and being open to collaboration. For example, a Gen Zer might negotiate for flexible working hours or purpose-driven projects, not just pay.

How Gen Zers Are Bringing New Approaches

Purpose Over Perks: Job or project negotiations are just as likely to focus on meaningful work and inclusion as they are on salary and benefits.

Digital Influences: Gen Z's fluency with digital platforms means they may use new tools or media but also face unique challenges (like negotiating through screens without face-to-face cues).

Relationship Focus: They often value ongoing relationships and community impact, and not just one-off gains, which aligns strongly with value-based thinking.

Self-Advocacy and Empowerment: Gen Z is less likely to accept unfair situations, using negotiation to demand respect, flexibility, and alignment with personal values, even in early-career roles.

Tips for Gen Zers (and Those Supporting Them)

- Learn negotiation as a core life skill, not just for business, but for all life scenarios.
- Practice separating your needs (interests) from your wants (positions).
- Prepare in advance by knowing what you stand for and what you're willing (or not willing) to compromise on.
- Use collaboration, not confrontation, when seeking solutions that benefit all parties whenever possible.
- Emphasise shared values, highlight areas of agreement, and common goals.

Negotiation for Gen Z is rapidly evolving, becoming more values-driven, relational, and purposeful. By blending negotiation techniques with strong self-awareness and a focus on genuine values, Gen Zers are making their mark in the workplace and beyond.

Real Life Example

A job seeker is offered a position with a company, but feels the starting salary isn't sufficient. Instead of accepting the initial offer, they negotiate by highlighting their skills, sharing research on industry salaries, and respectfully requesting a higher starting pay and some remote work flexibility. The employer considers their value and agrees to both an increased salary and a hybrid work schedule. As a result, the job seeker is happier and more productive, while the employer gains a motivated, satisfied employee. This outcome would not have been possible without the candidate's effective negotiation; both sides benefited more than if the initial offer had been accepted without negotiation.

Exercise

1. For one week, write down every instance where you needed to 'negotiate' - however small.
2. This could include:
   - Asking for deadline extensions
   - Discussing chores or household responsibilities
   - Splitting bills or rides
   - Handling returns, refunds, or customer service

> - Any situation where you tried to influence an outcome
> 3. Pick one of the examples you identified and reflect on the following:
>   - What went well? How did you manage to negotiate the required outcome
>   - What could have improved? Did you miss an opportunity? Could you have communicated more clearly? Did you avoid saying something you wanted to say?
>   - What will you do differently next time to negotiate the outcome in a better way?

We live in a period of economic uncertainty. Learning how to adapt to changes in the job market, lifelong learning, and upskilling become essential. The next chapter discusses thriving in uncertain times.

Thriving in Uncertain Times

12

THRIVING IN UNCERTAIN TIMES

Coping with Economic Uncertainty & Job Market Shifts

Gen Z has come of age during a time of significant change, marked by events such as Brexit, the COVID-19 pandemic, economic upheaval, and rapid technological advancements. For young people, 'uncertainty' isn't just a buzzword, but a daily reality, like student loans, unpredictable job prospects, and a gig economy where traditional job security is rare. Rather than chasing the illusion of complete stability, thriving involves learning to anticipate, accept, and adapt to change.

Coping with uncertainty professionally may involve developing flexibility around job roles or industry sectors. Financially, it means maintaining an emergency fund to handle brief disruptions. Emotionally, it's about cultivating a growth mindset: viewing setbacks as opportunities for learning rather than failures. Many young people now anticipate career pivots, periods of freelancing, or returning to training throughout their working lives. Making peace with 'not knowing' isn't resignation, it's empowerment.

The Importance of Lifelong Learning & Upskilling

The half-life of skills is shrinking quickly; what you learn today is likely to need updating in just a few years' time. Lifelong learning isn't just an option; it's essential to stay flexible in the face of automation and changing market demands. The UK provides many routes for upskilling, from free platforms like **FutureLearn** and the Open University to paid courses on **Coursera** or **Udemy**. Many employers - especially in tech, digital marketing and health- value proven commitment to ongoing learning even more than formal degrees.

Micro-credentials, bootcamps, and digital badges can effectively enhance a CV. Whether it's sharpening your coding, data analysis, communication, or leadership skills, actively dedicating time to learning yields significant benefits. Flexible workers stand out and are more resilient because they are better prepared to seize new opportunities as industries change.

Balancing Ambition with Mental & Emotional Health

Ambition drives growth, but if left unchecked, it can lead to burnout. Gen Z is often viewed as ambitious and entrepreneurial, but mental health statistics reveal a more complex picture: record numbers reporting stress, anxiety, and depression, worsened by the pressure to 'do it all' and the endless comparisons encouraged by social media. Learning to appreciate psychological safety alongside achievement is now crucial.

Building routines that support wellbeing, such as regular sleep, exercise, healthy eating, and breaks from digital overload, lays the foundation for sustainable ambition. Seeking support through NHS mental health services, university or workplace schemes, or charities like Mind can make a significant difference. Setting boundaries (like saying no or limiting side hustle overwork), practising mindfulness, and establishing supportive peer or mentor networks all help to balance drive with self-care.

Real Life Examples

Example 1: Career Pivot After Redundancy

Tom, aged 24, from Liverpool, was made redundant from his hospitality job during the pandemic. Instead of viewing this as a permanent setback, he explored online learning and enrolled in a free digital marketing course. Six months later, he began freelancing by managing social media for local businesses - discovering a new passion and a more stable income. His adaptability transformed a crisis into an opportunity.

Example 2: Building a Resilience Toolkit

Harriet, finishing university in Edinburgh, felt paralysed by job market anxiety. She began structuring her week with routines: daily walks, virtual study groups, and check-ins with friends. She created a 'resilience checklist' (favourite podcasts, calming techniques, people to call) for tough days. When rejected from multiple applications, she reflected on what she had learned, adjusted her approach, and eventually secured a graduate job.

Exercises

1. Resilience Toolkit Creation
- List five activities or strategies that help you stay calm or focused in tough times (e.g., meditation, speaking with a mentor, exercise, journaling).
- Add at least two emergency contacts or support lines (such as the Samaritans, Mind, colleague support, local NHS helplines).
- Keep your toolkit somewhere accessible and refer to it whenever you feel overwhelmed.

2. Self-Care and Wellbeing Checklist
- For one week, track your sleep, exercise, social interaction, and downtime.
- At week's end, reflect: What energised you? What left you drained? Are you prioritising rest as much as productivity?
- Commit to one new self-care habit, however small, for the following month.

3. Lifelong Learning Challenge
- Identify one new skill you want to learn or improve (e.g., Excel spreadsheets, basic coding, public speaking).
- Research one free/affordable UK-based online course or tutorial to get started.
- Share your goal with a peer or accountability group; review progress after four weeks.

4. Ambition-Balance Reflection
- Write down your top three ambitions for the next year.
- For each, list possible obstacles and strategies for maintaining balance (e.g., taking a break

> after major milestones, reaching out for feedback/support).
> - Reflect on occasions when you might need to slow down or change course, and permit yourself to do so, if needed.

You're not an island. We live in a community, a country, and a world where we all need to coexist. The next chapter explores the ideas of ethical investing, conscious consumerism, and social entrepreneurship.

Money, Ethics, & Social Good

13

MONEY, ETHICS, & SOCIAL GOOD

Ethical Investing, Conscious Consumerism, & Social Entrepreneurship

The way we handle our money sends strong signals about our values and priorities. Ethical investing is becoming increasingly popular among Gen Z, as young people want their savings and pensions to help create a more sustainable and just world. Ethical or ESG (Environmental, Social, Governance) funds let you invest in companies dedicated to low-carbon solutions, fair labour practices, and social justice. It involves examining not just the financial return, but also the impact of the businesses you support, avoiding harmful industries while encouraging positive change.

Conscious consumerism applies this mindset to everyday life: every pound spent acts as a vote for the kind of business practices you support. Purchasing from local, minority-owned, or B Corp-certified brands shows concern for social and environmental issues. Quick online research or ethical shopping apps can reveal how brands perform on transparency, waste reduction, or fair employment. Social entrepreneurship takes values even further, as young founders create mission-driven businesses to address issues like food waste, youth unemployment, or digital inclusion, combining profit with purpose. In essence, '**Think global, act local.**'

Giving Back: Volunteering, Philanthropy, and Activism

An increasing number of UK Gen Zers dispute the idea that making a difference requires significant wealth. Volunteering, whether at a local foodbank, climate action group, or digital skills collective, can be just as valuable (sometimes more) as making regular donations. Philanthropy isn't exclusive to millionaires; even small contributions to community crowdfunding or charity appeals are important.

Digital activism enables young people to support causes worldwide - organising campaigns, pressuring brands for change, or joining mutual aid networks. The common theme is recognising that individual actions, when combined, generate collective pressure for systemic change. 'Giving back' is becoming a regular part of financial planning, with some young people allocating a fixed percentage of their income to good causes.

How to Spot 'Greenwashing'

With the rise of ethical consumerism, some companies try to improve their image with misleading environmental claims, known as 'greenwashing'. Recognising vague language (such as 'eco-friendly', 'green', 'all-natural') and seeking out strong certifications (like Fairtrade, Soil Association, FSC) is important. Companies that openly publish impact reports, supply chain audits, or third-party certifications are generally more trustworthy.

Researching brand reputations is easier than ever: independent watchdogs, review apps, and social media quickly expose poor practices. Making informed choices involves pausing before buying, checking sources, and asking: Does this company's impact match its advertising? Incorporating ethics into your money routine doesn't mean perfection - just mindful improvement, step by step.

Real Life Examples

Example 1: Investing for Impact

Leah, a 24-year-old teacher in Leeds, wanted her pension to reflect her climate values. She used her workplace pension portal to switch funds, choosing one that excluded fossil fuels and prioritised renewable energy. She encouraged her colleagues to do the same, feeling empowered that her retirement savings supported causes she believed in.

Example 2: Community Volunteering & Side Hustle Synergy

Jake, a Birmingham university student, ran a small online vintage clothing shop. Inspired by activism on Instagram, he dedicated 5% of profits to a local homelessness charity and volunteered at fundraising events. His social enterprise model attracted like-minded customers and collaborators, enabling him to combine business, community, and impact.

Exercises

1. Values-Based Spending Plan

- Identify your three core ethical values (e.g., sustainability, fairness, innovation).
- Review your last month of bank/card statements & tally spending by category - does your outflow match these values, or are there disconnects?

- Set two concrete goals (e.g., switch to a green energy provider, buy second-hand fashion for one month).

2. Spot the Greenwash

- Gather three product adverts claiming to be 'eco,' 'natural,' or 'carbon neutral.'
- Investigate each: Are there third-party certifications? Is the supply chain transparent? What do independent reviewers say?
- Decide: If the company backs up its claims, or is it just marketing?

3. Social Impact Brainstorm

- List three causes you care about.
- For each, note one way to give back - donate time, skills, money, or advocacy.
- Share your commitment online or with a group for accountability.

4. Giving Back Tracker

- Set a goal to contribute either a percentage of your monthly earnings or a set number of volunteering hours.
- Use a spreadsheet or app to log contributions (financial and time-based) across the year.
- Reflect quarterly: How has giving back affected your outlook, community, or skills?

It may seem a lifetime away, but you, too, will age like your parents and grandparents. Planning for this stage is wise, and in fact, time is a powerful advantage for Gen Z. The next chapter will show you how to leverage starting early with retirement planning and leaving a legacy.

The Future - Retirement & Legacy

14

THE FUTURE - RETIREMENT & LEGACY

Why Future Planning Isn't Just for 'Old People'

Imagine your future self: what kind of lifestyle do you want decades from now? Planning for retirement and your legacy isn't about being morbid or boring; it's about giving *yourself* choices and freedom later on, not just scraping by. With the odds stacked against most Gen Z in the UK (like high house prices, gig work, and hefty student loans), taking early action can put you ahead.

Thinking Retirement Is Too Far Away

Many Gen Zers regularly push retirement savings down the priority list, often waiting for a mythical 'better time' or assuming an inheritance will sort it all out. However, relying on inheritance is a risky bet - life expectancy is rising, living costs are up, and what's left to inherit might be a lot less than you think, especially with possible changes to inheritance tax and long-term care needs.

Why Start Now?

- **Automatic Enrolment (AE):** Most UK employees are now automatically enrolled in a workplace pension. However, remember that sticking to the minimum is unlikely to suffice in 2025; a median earner at the minimum AE will only end up with roughly £158,000 in a pension pot, worth approximately £13,000 per year (excluding the State Pension), which is far short of the ideal for a comfortable retirement.

Don't Count Only on the State Pension

The State Pension remains an important safety net, but it won't fully fund the life you dream about. In the 2025-26 tax year, the full new State Pension is £230.25 per week (about £11,973 per year), and this is only available if you've paid enough years of National Insurance. Most people need more to cover essentials, housing, travel, and health expenses. If your annual outgoings are £25,000, you'll need other savings or investments to cover the gap.

Secure Your Future: Multiple Income Streams

Depending on just one income source (like the State Pension) is risky. Diversify across:

- **Workplace & Private pensions:** Take full advantage, especially matching employer contributions.

- **Investments:** Build a portfolio—**Stocks & Shares ISAs**, **SIPP**, or **robo-advisors** to grow wealth tax-efficiently

- **Side hustles and property:** Rental income, freelance gigs, or small businesses add flexibility and income in retirement.

- **Consolidation** is essential: Having multiple short-term jobs can leave you with numerous 'mini' pension pots scattered around, so consider consolidating them to avoid losing savings and paying unnecessary charges. This is where keeping proper records becomes very important. Companies often merge or are acquired, making it hard to know where a pot is at any given time.

Think Beyond Money—Leave a Legacy

Future planning isn't just about you. Creating a will, nominating pension beneficiaries, and specifying who receives what (including digital assets) can make life easier for those you love.

Real Life Example

Example 1

Sophie, a 28-year-old mid-generation Gen Zer working in digital marketing, began seriously considering her financial future. Instead of relying solely on her pension from work, Sophie set up a stocks and shares ISA and began contributing monthly. She regularly checks her pension statements, increases contributions when she gets a pay raise, and uses budgeting apps to track progress.

By investing early and taking advantage of tax-efficient options, Sophie is building a solid foundation for retirement while maintaining flexibility for life's changes. This forward-thinking approach helps her feel secure about her future and confident that she'll have financial independence later in life.

Example 2

Alan, age 55, works as a civil engineer in Manchester. Having started pension contributions in his thirties, Alan reviews his retirement plan annually with a financial adviser. He has consistently topped up his workplace pension, moved some savings into a tax-efficient ISA, and paid off most of his mortgage. Alan is now considering part-time work as retirement approaches and has begun thinking about when to access his pension pot. By staying proactive and updating his plan, he ensures a smoother transition to retirement, with financial security and more freedom to enjoy his later years.

CONCLUSION

As Gen Z, you're coming of age during an extraordinary time of transformation. The world of work, money and personal meaning is shifting faster than ever. Yet change offers as many opportunities as it does uncertainties. This book has guided you through the foundational skills and mindsets necessary to thrive, from reframing your attitude towards money to building practical financial literacy to aligning your money with your values. In this concluding summary, we highlight the key truths to carry with you as you chart your own course.

1. There's No One 'Right' Route - Success Is Personal

The traditional path: typically, school, university, a lifelong job, and a mortgage, has changed. Some will find fulfilment through university and professional careers, while others will find it through apprenticeships, side hustles, or entrepreneurial ventures. Success is personal. What matters most is aligning your journey with your interests, strengths, values, and life circumstances. Challenge outdated myths: a high salary or a particular postcode does not guarantee happiness or security. Only you can define what fulfilment means for yourself - and this definition can (and should) change over time.

2. Mindset and Habits Trump Short-Term Wins

We've seen how powerful your 'money mindset' is - shaped by upbringing, culture, and the scroll of social media feeds. Lasting security isn't about making a quick buck, but about building self-awareness, adaptability, and healthy financial habits. Whether you're budgeting, saving, or investing, small, consistent actions - starting now, no matter how modest - compound into substantial progress. Be prepared to learn, make mistakes, and adjust. Remember, resilience - bouncing back from setbacks and learning to adapt - is one of your greatest assets.

3. Financial Literacy Is Empowerment

Understanding the fundamentals: how to budget, the mechanics of debt and credit in the UK, the power of compound interest, and the landscape of investing, empowers you in a world filled with noise and misinformation. You don't need to be 'rich' to begin; you simply need information, intention, and curiosity. Plenty of tools are available: digital banks, straightforward investment apps, online courses, and support communities. Seek out trustworthy sources, ask questions, and remain cautious of 'guaranteed' shortcuts - especially in the era of viral scams.

4. The World of Work Is Flexible - and Demands Flexibility

Gone are the days when a single job could guarantee lifelong security. The gig economy, digital platforms, and the rise of AI mean new types of work and income are constantly emerging. Learn to future-proof yourself: invest in skills that machines can't replicate - creativity, empathy, critical thinking. Don't be afraid to pivot or try new things, from side hustles to new learning experiences. Networking, building your brand, and maintaining a flexible mindset are key to navigating unpredictable changes.

5. Money and Meaning Can Go Hand In Hand

Aligning your finances with your ethics and values enhances both your well-being and the wider world. Ethical investing, conscious consumerism, volunteering, and social entrepreneurship are no longer niche pursuits; they are core ways many Gen Zers lead fulfilled lives. Reflect on how your spending, saving, and even earning, influence society and the planet around you. Small steps, multiplied by millions, address injustice, combat climate change, and foster a sense of community. Your money is a tool for personal security and global impact.

6. Well-being is the Foundation

All ambitions in the world mean little without the physical and mental health to enjoy them. Prioritise self-care, rest, and supportive relationships. Know when to switch off, when to reach out, and when to permit yourself to change direction. Achievement is most rewarding when balanced with meaning, connection, and a sense of inner security.

As you progress, remember that **adaptability, curiosity, and values-driven choices** are your greatest assets. The future isn't something you merely inherit; it's something you shape, one decision at a time. Stay open-minded, keep learning, invest in yourself and your community, and never stop questioning what truly matters to you. The journey is uniquely yours, and it's only just beginning.

FURTHER READING BY TOPIC

Money Mindset

- **"The Psychology of Money: Timeless lessons on wealth, greed, and happiness" by Morgan Housel**
    - Roadmap for transforming your relationship with money and achieving financial independence.

- **"Happy Money: The Science of Smarter Spending" by Elizabeth Dunn & Michael Norton**
    - Explores the link between money and happiness based on psychological research.

- **"The Compound Effect: Jumpstart Your Income" by Darren Hardy**

Financial Literacy & Basics

- **"The Meaningful Money Handbook" by Pete Matthew (UK-focused)**
    - Covers budgeting, financial planning, and investing for beginners.

- **Moneyhelper (UK website)**
    - Free guides on budgeting, saving, debt, banking, and credit.

Earning in the New Economy

- **"Side Hustle: From Idea to Income in 27 Days" by Chris Guillebeau**
  - Step-by-step guide for creating side income streams.
  - **UK Gov's "Working for yourself"**
  - Information on tax, legal status, and practicalities for gig and freelance work.

Investing for Beginners

- **"Investing Demystified" by Lars Kroijer (UK)**
  - Focus on index funds, diversification, and starting small.
- **MoneySavingExpert's Investing Guide**
  - Beginner-friendly, UK-focused online resource.

Career Paths & Skills

- **"So Good They Can't Ignore You" by Cal Newport**
  - Why skills and experience often trump passion in building fulfilling careers.
- **"The Squiggly Career" by Helen Tupper & Sarah Ellis (UK)**
  - Navigating nonlinear, portfolio careers with practical exercises.
- **LinkedIn Learning / Coursera / FutureLearn**

- Find free/affordable courses tailored to your chosen field.

Money, Ethics, and Social Good

- **"The Ethical Investor: How to Quit Toxic Companies and Grow Your Wealth" by Nicole Haddow**
  - Practical guide on making your investments align with personal ethics.

Staying Up to Date

- **Podcasts:** "The Financial Diet," "Money Clinic" (by the FT), "Girls That Invest," "Make Money Equal"
- **Websites/Forums:** r/UKPersonalFinance (Reddit), Boring Money, Young Money Blog, LinkedIn Groups by industry

Final Encouragement

Remember, your journey continues: this reading list and action guide are only the start. Explore broadly, question deeply, connect with others, and adapt as the world evolves. Each step forward, no matter how small, builds confidence and creates new opportunities for your future.

BOOK REVIEW REQUEST

If you found this book helpful, pay it forward by leaving a review of one or more of the following:
- **Goodreads.com, Your Reading Diary**
- **Amazon: The Literary Marketplace**
- **BookBub: The Book Lover's Hub**
- **Instagram: A Picture-Perfect Review**
- **Facebook Reader Groups: Join the Conversation**
- **Your Local Bookstores: Support Offline Communities**
- **Or email me your review so I can post it for you.**

Others who have not discovered this resource will appreciate it.

TITLES IN THE 'EYES-WIDE-OPEN' SERIES

Navigating the Digital Maze: Social Media, Technology & You

Step into the fast-paced world of digital life with this essential guide for Gen Z. Navigating the Digital Maze examines the influence of social media, technology, and online trends, offering practical strategies for building a healthy digital identity, managing screen time, and staying safe online. Featuring real-life stories, interactive challenges, and expert advice, this book empowers you to take charge of your digital world and flourish both online and offline.

Real Talk: Mental Health in a Connected World

Mental health matters now more than ever, and Real Talk is your go-to companion for navigating the pressures of modern life. Discover how to manage stress, build resilience, and foster genuine connections in an always-on society. Packed with relatable stories, actionable self-care tips, and stigma-busting exercises, this book helps you prioritise your wellbeing and support others on the journey to mental wellness.

How To Thrive in Life

Imagine for a moment that your life is a blank book, where you're both the author and the main character. Each day, you write a new page, sometimes with excitement, sometimes with uncertainty, but always with the power to choose what happens next. This book aims to support you in making those choices with confidence, courage, and kindness. Although you can't control everything that occurs, you can decide how you respond, what you learn, and how you grow. This is your life. This book will help make it extraordinary.

All of Us: Diversity, Inclusion & Finding Your Place

Celebrate what makes you unique and discover the power of community in All of Us. This book explores identity, empathy, and belonging in a diverse world, guiding you through the challenges of stereotypes, exclusion, and allyship. With interactive exercises and real-world stories, you will learn how to build inclusive spaces, advocate for others, and find your place in a changing society.

Voices of Change: Activism, Values & Building a Better World

Your voice matters, and Voices of Change demonstrates how to harness it. Immerse yourself in the realm of youth activism, from discovering your cause to constructing movements and making a significant impact. Investigate innovative strategies, ethical activism, and the resilience required to effect genuine change. Both inspiring and practical, this book serves as your guide to transforming values into action and shaping a brighter future.

Heart to Heart: Navigating Personal Relationships in Modern Times

Unlock the secrets to meaningful connections with Heart to Heart. Whether you're forming friendships, navigating romance, or establishing boundaries, this guide provides honest advice and interactive tools for every stage of your relationship journey. Learn to communicate with confidence, resolve conflicts, and grow together in a world where relationships matter more than ever.

ABOUT THE AUTHOR

James is the father of two grown children, a stepfather to three others, and a grandfather to seven more. Therefore, he has a lot at stake. His only wish is for all children, teenagers, and adults to thrive in life, regardless of their background, beliefs, or values.

He began writing fifteen years ago, creating books that appeal to the inner child in all adults and feature very British humour - **The Hole Trilogy**. He continued his creative journey by writing an eight-book series for children aged 7 to 9 years old - **The Billy Growing Up Series**. These stories are traditional, addressing negative behaviours with positive outcomes for children.

The **Eyes-Wide-Open Series** for Gen Zers grew out of his appreciation for the rapid changes affecting the world and observing how upcoming generations, like us all, are struggling to make sense of what is happening around them.

SOCIAL MEDIA
Websites

www.jamesminter.com

www.billygrowingup.com

E-mail:
james@jamesminter.com

X: @james_minter

Instagram:
instagram.com/james_minter_author/

Facebook
facebook.com/eyes-wide-open

facebook.com/author.james.minter

ACKNOWLEDGEMENTS

Like all projects of this type, several indispensable individuals assist in bringing them to completion. These include my wife, Maggie, who patiently endures my endless requests to read, comment on, and discuss my story. She also contributes editorially to the insights designed to support Gen Zers in becoming responsible adults through her role as a personal development coach. In addition, I am grateful to a circle of trusted friends and colleagues whose honest feedback, encouragement, and diverse perspectives have helped refine my ideas and ensure the content remains relevant and impactful for young readers. Their collective expertise, spanning digital literacy, mental health, and diversity, has been invaluable in shaping a resource that meets the real-world needs of Gen Z. Without their unwavering support and commitment, this project would not have achieved its current depth and clarity.

www.ingramcontent.com/pod-product-compliance
Lightning Source LLC
Chambersburg PA
CBHW011127070526
44584CB00028B/3805